Managing Winning Proposals

Preparing a proposal for a contract or a grant can be an overwhelming and extraordinarily complex process, but regardless of the proposal type or sector, certain truths always pertain.

This book walks the proposal manager through the steps that are essential and common to every single proposal and ensure a foundation for winning. Many proposal management books are of little use, particularly to a first-time proposal manager, owing to their broad scope and unrealistic assumptions about resources, including time, expertise and information. This book provides actionable, concrete steps for the activities that underpin all successful proposals, providing a step-by-step description of how to make a proposal compliant and compelling. The premise of this book, based on the author's hands-on experience in multiple proposal roles for over three decades, is that proposals do not go off the rails owing to an inability to implement advanced techniques and complicated processes. They fail because of inattention to fundamental activities. Other business books cover some of these fundamental activities. However, proposals differ because of their tight constraints: deadlines, the need for perfect compliance with detailed instructions, fierce competition for limited funds, the consequences of not winning and the stress that inevitably accompanies the process. Focusing solely on the preparation of the written proposal document and not on sales, negotiation, marketing, or customer interaction, this book dives into the details of the tasks facing the person actually accountable and responsible for the preparation and delivery of the proposal.

Proposal managers of all levels, from first-timers to seasoned pros looking to polish their skills, as well as those who participate in the proposal process but are not intimately familiar with it – artists, technical writers, project managers, accountants and others – will benefit from the processes and tools described in this book.

Wendy Frieman has been writing and managing proposals for over three decades, is accredited at the highest levels by both the APMP and the NCMA and is the only professional who has been elected a Fellow by both organizations. She also holds undergraduate and graduate degrees from Stanford University.

Managing Winning Proposals

The Fundamentals

Wendy Frieman

Routledge
Taylor & Francis Group
NEW YORK AND LONDON

Designed cover image: 24 Hour Company – Design to Win

First published 2026
by Routledge
605 Third Avenue, New York, NY 10158

and by Routledge
4 Park Square, Milton Park, Abingdon, Oxon, OX14 4RN

Routledge is an imprint of the Taylor & Francis Group, an informa business

Library of Congress Cataloging-in-Publication Data
Names: Frieman, Wendy author
Title: Managing winning proposals : the fundamentals / Wendy Frieman.
Description: New York, NY : Routledge, 2025. | Includes bibliographical references and index. |
Identifiers: LCCN 2025000822 (print) | LCCN 2025000823 (ebook) | ISBN 9781032947334 hardback | ISBN 9781032947327 paperback | ISBN 9781003581475 ebook
Subjects: LCSH: Requests for proposals (Public contracts)
Classification: LCC HD3860 .F85 2025 (print) | LCC HD3860 (ebook) | DDC 352.5/3—dc23/eng/20250328
LC record available at https://lccn.loc.gov/2025000822
LC ebook record available at https://lccn.loc.gov/2025000823

ISBN: 9781032947334 (hbk)
ISBN: 9781032947327 (pbk)
ISBN: 9781003581475 (ebk)

DOI: 10.4324/9781003581475

Typeset in Sabon
by codeMantra

Contents

Introduction

The motivation to write this book stems from my desire to share insights about proposal management after decades of experience and observation. It is also driven by a commitment to people new to the proposal management profession to explain the steps that are essential to every single proposal, whether for a government contract, a foundation grant or a contract with a commercial organization. These apply regardless of the level of complexity of the request for proposal (RFP), the customer, the industry, the discipline, the number of pages or the duration. They apply whether the proposal team is one person or 100 people, whether the bidder is selling lawn-mower parts, algorithms to support rocket propulsion technology, armed guard services or enrichment programs for disabled children. Furthermore, they can be used for any document that has to contain specific information, in a pre-defined format, with a deadline. It will work for a homework assignment, an essay contest or a college application. You can also use these steps for sole source proposals (acquisitions that are not competitive) and grants that are awarded on a "rolling admissions" basis, both of which it is important to complete according to the instructions.

Executing these steps does not guarantee that you will succeed. But ignoring them or neglecting to take them seriously puts you at a much higher risk for failure. In other words, they are always necessary, if not always sufficient.

Context and History

Before defining the fundamentals, it is useful to look back on why proposal management has become a profession. It is certainly a new profession compared with law, medicine, finance or academia. However, proposals have been in existence for over a century, even if they have had different names: tenders, bids, applications, requests. Local governments prepared proposals to get access to federal dollars, and scholars prepared proposals to

DOI: 10.4324/9781003581475-1

get grants to support their research. Companies wrote proposals to the federal government to supply goods and services. In the US, prior to 1985, most federal government contracts were awarded without competition by means of "sole source" acquisitions. Government officials would decide on the most qualified provider and then ask that company to prepare a proposal. When the US Congress passed the 1985 Competition in Contracting Act (CCA), sole source or non-competitive proposals became the exception rather than the rule in US federal contracting; virtually all contracts above a minimal threshold had to be awarded competitively. Because of the amount of money spent on federal contracts (today over $700 billion), the US Congress put in place laws and regulations to ensure that contracts were being awarded to companies who had proven, through competition, that they offered the best value.

All of a sudden, proposals became much more important because companies were not guaranteed contracts; they had to compete for them. Revenues, profits and jobs all depended on a company's ability to prepare a compelling proposal. Companies began to form proposal departments and allocate budgets to support proposal development. Initially, companies staffed these departments with system engineers, administrative assistants, graphic artists and desktop publishers. Proposal teams within the same company had different schedules and tools, many of which were improvised and subject to change. But, over time, because of the expense of proposal preparation and the high stakes involved, it became clear that responding to a request for proposal (RFP) required a repeatable process. The proposal management process was born. The shift away from sole source to competitive acquisitions resulted in changes for government procurement officials as well. Many of them had no experience in writing competitive RFPs or evaluating proposals from multiple companies for the same acquisition.

Since 1985, many US state and local governments have followed the lead of the federal government when buying goods and services. Corporations operate in a different environment, and the regulations that dictate how they buy products and services vary depending on size and equity structure. The vast majority of significant acquisitions by large US companies use a competitive bid process. They, after all, have the same type of obligation to their shareholders that the US government has to US taxpayers. A similar evolution took place in US universities, many of which now receive millions of dollars from the federal government for research, and many of which have their own proposal departments. Proposal management followed a similar trajectory in many other countries, although the terminology often differs. The Association for Proposal Management Professionals, which grew from a few hundred people in the 1980s and now has more than 10,000 members, has 13 chapters outside the US.

Whether in government, academia or corporations, competitive acquisitions share some basic attributes. They entail rules that all the bidders must follow. They include instructions that describe the specific content of the proposal, as well as the format. Most have a single deadline that all bidders must meet. These features make it easier for evaluators to compare one vendor's proposal with another's, and the deadlines exist to make it fair, so that no one vendor has an advantage in the bidding process.

For someone who has never read an RFP, the job of preparing a proposal seems simple: just follow the instructions and submit the proposal on time. What is hard about that? The answer is, many things make it hard:

- Proposals typically require information and insights from multiple sources, and often the information is in someone's head and has never been written down. Often, the people who are the most capable of writing the proposal have many competing demands on their time. Or, the person with the most knowledge of the topic is not a good writer;
- RFPs often include strict rules on the format and length of the proposal. The need for accuracy and completeness is extreme; sometimes, a small clerical error can result in a proposal being disqualified;
- Promises and commitments in proposals often become legally binding upon award, so the content has to be carefully scrutinized by the teams who will be in charge of executing the work;
- Proposal teams have imperfect information about competitors and underlying customer concerns and attitudes, so they write generic content;
- Time pressure and conflicting priorities can cause even senior professionals to act irrationally, introduce errors, avoid critical decisions and alienate colleagues whose cooperation is essential to the process;
- Electronic and physical delivery of the proposal are subject to weather, traffic, network congestion, personal emergencies and national emergencies, and late proposals are almost always immediately disqualified;
- The solicitations themselves are often ambiguous, especially if they are written by committee, and if they contain multiple sections, regulations, specifications and technical details. Sometimes bidders can clear up ambiguities through a question-and-answer process, but often they have to make interpretations and assumptions.

Sole source proposals are inherently less challenging because the bidder has no competition. They still require attention to detail and adherence to deadlines. Many grant applications get submitted on a rolling basis and do not have strict deadlines, but professionals and scholars who prepare grant applications encounter many of the same challenges as proposal teams in industry. For everyone, therefore, the process is almost never easy or simple.

Why This Book Was Necessary

Many, many tools and processes now exist to navigate the challenges in the bidding on a competitive RFP. Multiple books, articles, webinars and courses exist to explain all tools and processes. So, why another book on the topic? Because, along the way, many of us in the profession have become enamored of the terms and the methodologies and the software and have lost sight of the basics. We went to proposal university and got a PhD in proposals. We invented more and more tools and processes. We developed our own language to talk about proposals: "action captions," "win themes," "discriminators," "black hats" and many more. I am a firm believer in repeatable processes and in using language consistently, and I myself have participated in the creation of proposal tools. But not all tools and processes are necessary or useful for every proposal. Some are difficult to use and time-consuming. Some are nice-to-haves; others are critical. How does someone just starting out know what is essential and what is optional?

That is one reason this book was necessary. It is only about the non-optional. It is not about the specifics of the process each organization uses to prepare and review proposals, often defined as "red teams," "win themes," "strengths," "discriminators," or "storyboards," although I define these terms, because not all winning proposals started with storyboards or were reviewed by color teams. I am willing to take the slings and arrows of my friends and colleagues in the profession who will not agree with this statement. But I am writing this book because I have seen too many proposal teams spend time debating the merit of one win theme over another while ignoring proposal instructions and requirements. I have seen too many proposal professionals worry about action captions and discriminators without reading the RFP carefully enough to know that they should not be bidding in the first place. Someone who is new to the profession has no way to know, when reading all the literature we have generated, what is mission-critical and what is an advanced proposal technique not suitable for every bid.

A second reason for writing this book is the disconnect between what I read in our professional literature and the real-world conditions I encounter. Many of our processes, tools and templates assume the existence of perfect customer knowledge, deep understanding of competitor strengths and weaknesses, a well-defined and documented solution or offering, unlimited time, an army of skilled professionals standing at the ready, strong writers, the latest technology and a generous budget. One example comes from the Association of Proposal Management Professionals' (APMP) *Body of Knowledge*, which lists 12 items that should be prepared in advance of every kick-off meeting, including a work breakdown structure dictionary, writers' packages, a draft executive summary and a competitive analysis. Setting high standards for the proposals we manage is admirable. However, in the real world, proposal managers often cannot control the conditions or environment and therefore operate under very different conditions. Not infrequently, companies engage proposal managers at the last minute to respond to an RFP for which they are unprepared and that has a 10-day deadline. We often encounter teams with a poor understanding of their own products or services or skills, executives who insist on bidding with very little knowledge of the customer or the market, insufficient budgets, professionals who lack the skills for their assigned proposal roles, staff who are already over-taxed and cannot focus or outdated technology. It is not unlike a poker game in which you must play the hand you are dealt if you want to stay in the profession. For some, this is eternally frustrating; for others, it is a challenge that keeps it interesting. For someone less experienced, scaling down the many, many steps that constitute the ideal process is complicated. Either way, I address how to apply the fundamentals regardless of the environment so that proposal managers can be effective in less-than-ideal situations.

"We might not have time for all the steps we are supposed to put in our production plan since the proposal is due Thursday."

A third reason for writing this book is that, when proposal management literature does address the fundamentals, their treatment is often superficial and not commensurate with their importance. By contrast, books and articles in our profession devote a lot of space to bid strategy, negotiation, marketing, customer knowledge and competitive analysis. These are critical to a winning bid, but they are almost always outside the control or purview of the proposal manager. By the time we get assigned to manage a proposal, either the business development team has done their job or they have not. There is rarely anything the proposal manager can do about it, although I do present some ideas in Chapter 6. We have to muddle through.

The lack of attention to the fundamentals has mystified me for years, and the process of writing this book has helped me to solve the puzzle. These fundamentals are difficult to break down and explain in clear and concrete language. They are not bright, shiny objects or quick fixes. They take time. Moreover, they involve decisions and interactions that proposal teams often prefer to avoid, despite the risks of ignoring them. Therefore, even when you learn the fundamentals, you will encounter challenges in applying them. There will always be people on the team who think that a better process or the latest software can provide a shortcut.

Although the original intended audience for this book was the proposal manager, because it explains the basics, it will also be useful for anyone who is newly assigned to a role in the proposal process. This includes writers, pricing experts, reviewers, graphic artists, desktop publishers, engineers and other subject matter experts, business development professionals and administrative staff who support proposals.

For professionals who think they have mastered the basics, think again. It always helps to go back and practice the fundamentals. Basketball players do it, and so do ballet dancers. Anyone who is expert in a craft or discipline knows the importance of practicing basic skills. We never "master" them. We continue to hone them, practice them, refine them.

Proposal Fundamentals

The basic steps for all proposals are:

1. Carefully analyzing and fully understanding RFP instructions and requirements;
2. Clearly defining the offering, products, services or solution being proposed;
3. Creating a structured outline based on the RFP;
4. Assembling a team and making assignments to develop proposal content and perform other tasks;
5. Creating and enforcing a schedule;

6. Writing clear and compelling content;
7. Reviewing and revising content;
8. Producing and delivering the proposal;
9. Communicating with the team and tracking progress.

These steps might seem self-evident. Yet anyone with proposal experience knows that proposal teams do not always devote the time and energy necessary to complete each one of them. Lack of sufficient attention to one or more of these steps can result from time pressure, over-commitment of the people working on the proposal, assumptions that people on the team will execute the steps on their own without guidance or instruction, or some combination of these reasons. Specific examples illustrate the consequences of skipping over these fundamental activities (Table 0.1).

Table 0.1

Activity	*Why Teams Pay Insufficient or Misguided Attention to This*	*Risk*
Fully analyzing and understanding the instructions and requirements in the RFP	RFPs are boring and difficult to read carefully. When deadlines are tight, the first instinct is to start writing the proposal right away	Rushing through this step often results in many hours of re-work late in the process, or abandoning the proposal altogether
Clearly defining the offering, products, services or solution being proposed	It is easy to assume that the right product or service exists without checking to make sure. Digging into the details takes time and often requires expertise	The bidder might propose something that will be difficult or impossible to execute. Or the bidder finds out that a solution is not possible after a lot of effort on the proposal (sunk costs)
Creating a structured outline based on the RFP	A good outline can require multiple iterations, which take time. People have different mental filing systems, and there can be many opinions on how a proposal should be structured	Reorganizing a fully written document is much more difficult, and time-consuming, than reorganizing an outline
Assembling a team and making assignments to develop proposal content and perform other tasks	It is easy for contributors to misunderstand instructions, and it can be uncomfortable for a proposal manager to exercise authority and get firm commitments. People working on the proposal bring different assumptions about what a task entails	Even the shortest, smallest proposals involve contributions from multiple people. There can be many interdependencies, and one person's inability to contribute affects the entire effort

(Continued)

Table 0.1 (Continued)

Activity	*Why Teams Pay Insufficient or Misguided Attention to This*	*Risk*
Creating and enforcing a schedule	It is not always easy to know how long things take, and sticking to deadlines is not a normal instinct for many people	An unrealistic schedule can mean late delivery, which typically results in disqualification, high levels of stress and burnout, or both
Writing clear and compelling content	Tight deadlines often preclude the iterations and careful editing needed to deliver the right message. Often, subject matter experts who have limited writing skills are assigned as writers	Unclear writing puts a burden on the proposal evaluator. The goal is to make life easy for the evaluator
Reviewing and revising content	No one likes to get "constructive" feedback. Reviewing proposal content takes time, and yet multiple reviews are essential	Skipping the review process or cutting it short means sending in a proposal with errors or weaknesses that could have been eliminated

Proposal books and training address some of these topics, but often not in the depth that they deserve to be treated, given how important they are. As a result, proposal teams flounder, and proposal managers experience unprecedented levels of stress when the foundation is missing. Performing triage is an essential part of the proposal manager's job, and keeping the team focused on the essential tasks at the right moment in time is something that proposal managers learn through experience. I often have to step in and re-order priorities after seeing very smart people convene meetings to talk about win themes without having carefully reviewed the solicitation instructions and requirements. Why do some people want to design the proposal cover before addressing the fundamentals?

One reason is that, although proposal management is a profession, many people within the profession learn on the job and never take time to think about the process. Others take formal training and learn about a large number of tools and processes, but not how to apply them in different situations or how to trade off among them when time and resources are limited. It is particularly easy to skip over some of the fundamental planning steps. The instinct to "just get going" is powerful. It is hard to believe that the methodical planning and preparation steps are really worth the time and energy they consume. Yet it is exactly because a proposal deadline is unforgiving that these steps must occur early in the process. Without them, time will be wasted down the road, when there is not any time to waste. The saying "slow down to speed up" is always difficult to implement until people start to see the payoff of taking time to build the right framework.

Another reason it is easy to ignore or downplay these steps is that they are hard. Writing down exactly what people, equipment and methodologies you are proposing is much harder than talking about the cover art. Asking people to commit to deadlines and assignments is not easy, even where there is only one person preparing the proposal, in which case that person has to commit to him- or herself. Years of observing engineers, writers, graphic artists, scientists and other professionals sidestep the essential and gravitate to the easier tasks has taught me that people default to what they know how to do, what is close at hand and what they are comfortable doing. There are professional proposal managers who can explain what a win theme is in great detail but do not know what is in the solicitation. They write brilliant action captions but wait until it is too late to impose and enforce deadlines.

A third reason that teams ignore them is that many of these activities are collaborative and iterative. Cooperation can be difficult owing to fundamental disagreements about strategy, differing interpretations of the language of the solicitation, schedule conflicts or missing knowledge and information. It seems inefficient, because it often is. In the summer of 2020, when most proposal teams were still working remotely, collaboration posed additional challenges. Like collaboration, iterations take time and are not inherently efficient. However, they result in a better final product. Iterations take time.

Guide to Using This Book

This book is organized into chapters that align with each of the nine fundamental activities. In each one, I present a clear definition of the activity, the context (why it is important), the timing, the relevant roles, the basic steps in the process and where to go for more information or training. Wherever possible, I provide examples from actual solicitations, across different disciplines and industries, and answers to common challenges. In addition, for those who want to use more advanced proposal tools and processes, such as ghosting, I reference when they would best be applied and point to additional resources for those topics. Although many examples are drawn from US government proposals, the principles apply to most domains and industries. Each chapter stands on its own. However, many of the fundamentals are interdependent. People new to the profession will want to cross-reference or read the entire book.

This is not a book for those who bid on contracts for commodities, where all products that meet the specifications are essentially the same. Companies selling internet cabling, plastic sheeting or felt-tip markers will not be able to secure a sale based on the strength of a proposal. In those scenarios, the lowest price typically wins. The book is for competitors in a situation where a written proposal makes a difference. At the same time, no written proposal, by itself, can guarantee that the bidder will win.

A good proposal is necessary, but not sufficient in most situations. Relationships with the decision-makers and a competitive price are equally important. I do refer to both where they are particularly relevant, but they do no constitute separate chapters; sales and pricing are art forms unto themselves and are beyond the scope of this book.

This book does not include processes for creating the budget or price for the contract or grant. RFPs usually contain specific instructions for this, and they vary widely in size and complexity. There is no one process that applies in all settings. This book also does not include processes that only apply to oral proposals, such as presentation skills, rehearsals or creation of visuals. But all of the activities described are applicable and essential to the preparation of oral proposals.

It is important to remember that all practices and processes live in a context. Using them effectively results from practice and feedback. No magic bullet exists to ensure that it will be easy to create a winning proposal. **Because each RFP is unique, you will have to execute specific tasks that are not in this book.** But making sure that you master the fundamentals will enable you to put your time, energy and dollars into the activities that will have the highest payoff. The fundamentals provide the foundation of the house. They are not sufficient, but they are necessary. No one wants to live on the slab of concrete that is the foundation of a house, but no one wants to live in a house without a foundation.

Because this book is intended for proposal managers in many different settings, including universities, large and small companies and non-profits, some of the job titles of people involved in the proposal process might not be familiar or relevant. When I use the word "company" or "organization" in this book, I am referring to whoever is submitting the proposal. I am using the terms "contract" and "project" interchangeably. "Customer" or "buyer" is the individual or organization that is awarding the contract or grant. The term "senior executive" refers to someone who has the authority to make decisions about the price, the terms and conditions and the proposal content. The terms "capture manager" and "business development manager" describe someone who is close to the customer or has good customer knowledge and has been following the opportunity. Typically, this is the person to whom the proposal manager reports. "Subject matter experts" are people who have in-depth knowledge of the products or services being proposed; they might be engineers, lawyers, scientists, project managers, accountants, doctors or other professionals.

Finally, for those who are managing a proposal on their own, with no subject matter experts or business development executives, each chapter contains some tips on how to manage as a team of one. The principles and processes are the same, and it is possible to scale them down to one individual.

Chapter 1

Analyzing the Request for Proposals

Definition

Analysis of the RFP means a careful scrutiny of all the documentation provided by the customer about the contract or grant. A good RFP analysis separates the signal from the noise, since most RFPs contain a lot of boilerplate that will ultimately affect execution but might not be directly relevant to the proposal. It entails identifying inconsistencies, such as instructions in one part of the RFP that conflict with instructions in another section. It includes finding terms or requirements that are ambiguous or vague. It also includes finding requirements that pose risks, either the risk of not being able to win or the risk of not being able to execute the contract once awarded. The analysis forms the basis for sending questions to the customer and getting clarification or a revised RFP.

Why Is it Important?

The solicitation, or RFP, is the formal statement of what a customer wants to buy and how bidders should propose the product, system or service. For professional proposal managers, the RFP is the bible. Often they know entire paragraphs by heart. Careful attention to the solicitation early in the process is critical:

- Analysis of the RFP can reveal "show stoppers" or insurmountable obstacles before a company spends time and other precious resources on proposal preparation;
- It is often possible to resolve ambiguities, inconsistencies or inaccuracies in the RFP if they are uncovered early, whereas addressing them later can introduce changes across the proposal document;
- The RFP contains the information you need to schedule and staff the proposal effort;

DOI: 10.4324/9781003581475-2

- The evaluation criteria in the RFP determine how the proposal will be scored; US federal, state and local governments are almost always required by law to follow the evaluation information provided to all the bidders in the RFP.

For these reasons, analysis of the RFP is foundational. It is a necessary step on which subsequent activities depend. If it is not done thoroughly and carefully, teams and organizations lose precious time in revisions and reworkings. Moreover, RFP language is often incorporated directly into the contract after award, which means that bidders are often held to the RFP requirements as a matter of law. Failing to truly understand the solicitation means that the bidder is signing up to commitments without really knowing what they are. This represents a degree of risk that no organization wants to take.

When proposal teams start analyzing the solicitation as soon as it is published, they can accurately predict what types of resources they will need to complete the proposal, identify any inconsistencies between RFP sections and uncover requirements or terms that might make it impossible for the organization to either bid or execute the work. I have worked with proposal teams that discovered, three weeks after RFP release, that they could no longer use the subcontractor they were dependent on because of a clause buried in an obscure section no one bothered to read. I have seen proposal managers find out from the engineering team, very late in the game, that the information technology solution will not be acceptable to the customer because it will not pass stringent security standards. The longer an RFP is, the more pages, the more attachments, the more trapdoors you will find.

Despite this, proposal teams read quickly and often miss words, phrases, sentences and sometimes entire paragraphs that contain critical information. By the time they find them, it is often too late to change the proposal, address risks or clarify language.

Challenges

There are several reasons why reading and analyzing the RFP is difficult. First, RFPs are boring. You cannot read them the way you would read a book. If you start at the beginning of a 150-page RFP, your eyes will probably glaze over before the 25th page – if not sooner. Second, no one person has the background or knowledge to read and interpret the entire document. Third, careful reading requires the kind of time and attention to detail that most people do not cultivate and practice regularly. Fourth, everyone has cognitive biases when reading. People miss letters and words and think they see words that are not there if they expect to see them. Brain science has documented this,[1] but, if you do not believe it, try taking an online proofreading test.[2] It is very easy to skip over words or phrases that people do not want to see.

There are multiple ways to overcome each of these challenges. As with many other things that sound easy, reading the RFP is not at all easy. The harder something is, in my experience, the more important it is to have a formal process and be deliberate. That is why I have experimented with different processes over the years and developed a series of concrete steps.

When Does it Happen?

Analysis begins as soon as you receive a draft or final RFP. This activity typically precedes all the other proposal activity described in chapters 3-8. However, it can be iterative. IF the RFP changes over time through amendments, the analysis might have to be revisited later in the process.

Who Owns it?

The proposal manager should orchestrate the process, but many other experts participate.

Steps in the Process

Before executing the steps, it is important to know what is in a typical RFP and how to break it up into pieces. Solicitations typically contain multiple sections and types of information, each one written by a different part of the buying organization: the subject matter experts, the finance team, the legal advisors, the security department and often many others. For large acquisitions, solicitation documents often contain multiple attachments and can number in the hundreds of pages. In the United States, the Federal Acquisition Regulations (FAR) established a standard set of labels for government RFP sections. Not all agencies use these headings, but they are important because proposal professionals, books and articles often refer to "Section L" or "Section M."

US state and local governments do not follow the federal government format or labeling system, and commercial buyers use still different terminology. So, it is essential to analyze all the content and not look only for the sections that align with those in the box.

Section A – Solicitation/Contract Form
Section B – Supplies and Services and Price/Cost
Section C – Description/Specifications/Statement of Work
Section D – Packaging and Marking

Section E – Inspection and Acceptance
Section F – Deliveries or Performance
Section G – Contract Administration Data
Section H – Special Contract Requirements
Section I – Contract Clauses
Section J – List of Attachments
Section K – Representations, Certifications and Other Statements of Offerors
Section L – Instructions, Conditions and Notices to Offerors
Section M – Evaluation Factors for Award

Despite the differences between them, most solicitations contain the following categories of information:

- A description of the requirements for the work, the service or the product, often referred to in government RFPs as "Statement of Work," "Performance Work Statement," "Specifications," or "Scope";
- Instructions as to how to structure the proposal document, as well as how to format and deliver it;
- How to communicate with the customer;
- Instructions on the required content for each proposal section;
- Information as to how each section of the proposal will be evaluated;
- Terms and conditions that the winner will have to abide by after the contract is awarded, including laws and regulations, payment schedules and use of subcontractors or vendors;
- Forms that have to be filled in and sometimes signed by a corporate officer;
- Background information as to why the buyer is issuing a solicitation, who the current provider is;
- Spreadsheets or other forms for documenting the price of the offering.

All these types of information are relevant when preparing a proposal, and they are all in the solicitation for a reason. Each category will be relevant to the proposal process. Instructions and evaluation criteria drive the proposal organization, schedule and budget. Instructions affect how you staff and organize the proposal. Contract terms and conditions seem irrelevant until you understand how the terms you will have to live by during execution affect your solution and how you present it.

Analyzing the RFP entails 11 steps (see Figure 1.1).

Even if you are not permitted to ask questions during the bidding process (step 10), the analysis itself is critical.

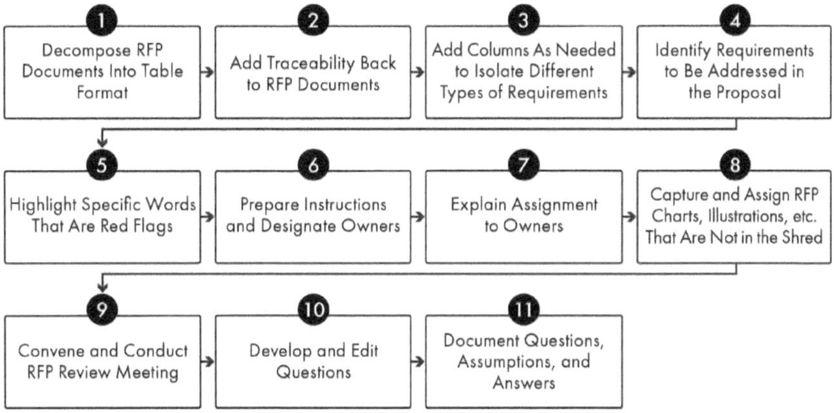

Figure 1.1 Analyzing the Solicitation

Step 1: Identify Experts and Decompose the RFP into Table Format

It is essential that a team of people scrutinize the RFP. No one person is going to be able to read and interpret the entire document. A subject matter expert in, for example, high energy physics, might not be able to identify contract terms and conditions that pose an unacceptable financial risk. Junior staff often do not have the experience to identify pricing constraints or assumptions that will make the bid non-competitive. Desktop publishers can find difficult formatting instructions. Engineers can assess the statement of work requirements. The legal or contracts team should scrutinize terms and conditions. Pricing experts are best positioned to understand spreadsheets and pricing models. The more people with different types of expertise analyze the RFP, the better understanding you will gain and the more you will lower the risk of an unpleasant surprise later on.

The standard practice is to email the RFP to the team and ask for comments. This rarely works! And not because people are lazy or incompetent. It is because working with RFPs is not something they do every day, not something they were trained to do and, quite possibly, not something they know how to do. No one trains, studies, practices or gets a degree in RFP analysis.

You will get better results from your team if you formalize the process and break down and format the RFP. In other words, to get results, it helps to spoon feed these experts and make their job as easy as possible.

That starts with the "stripping" process. Stripping simply means decomposing the RFP and converting text to table format so that each sentence is on one row of the table. Stripping the RFP makes it more digestible, especially if it is a long document, or it contains multiple documents, and requires many different types of expertise to fully understand. If your RFPs arrive in the form of a table or a checklist, you can skip this step. Most RFPs do not. They are more likely to contain paragraphs such as the following:

> Provide an overall Management Plan that identifies key personnel, the percentage of each person's time that will be committed to the project and describes the functions and responsibilities of each key person relative to the task to be performed. In addition, the management plan shall describe the experience of all key members. The Proposer must include a description of the organizational structure and management methodology used to provide service reliability and means of coordination and communication. The Management Plan shall identify the various staffing levels, including key managerial and supervisory personnel as well as office location and operational capabilities, for each area of the work as described in the Scope of Services. It shall clearly describe the functions and responsibilities of each staff member listed and Subcontractors/Subconsultants and include their experience relative to the tasks to be performed.

Reading text inside a paragraph inevitably means skipping over words and phrases. The human brain absorbs information much more easily when it arrives in "chunks." This is why it important to create a table so that each sentence is in its own cell. Compare the paragraph above with the same text formatted as a table.

Provide an overall Management Plan that identifies key personnel, the percentage of each person's time that will be committed to the project and describes the functions and responsibilities of each key person relative to the task to be performed.
In addition, the Management Plan shall describe the experience of all key members.
The Proposer must include a description of the organizational structure and management methodology used to provide service reliability and means of coordination and communication.
The Management Plan shall identify the various staffing levels, including key managerial and supervisory personnel as well as office location and operational capabilities, for each area of the work as described in the Scope of Services.
It shall clearly describe the functions and responsibilities of each staff member listed and Subcontractors/Subconsultants and include their experience relative to the tasks to be performed.

For most people, the table is a more readable format; when an RFP is deconstructed into a table, it is often referred to as a "shred." There are multiple ways to convert text into a table to create the shred. But you do not really need anything more than basic word processing software to create a requirements table, as long as you can convert your RFP into your word processing software. Do not try to convert a very large document all at once; break it into pieces.

Automated tools exist to create the shred. A tool can save time and minimize the possibility for human error. It is also true that automated tools are not perfect. If the tool does not capture every single requirement and there is one missing sentence in the proposal as a result, that alone can disqualify the proposal. So, any artifact that is generated using an automated tool has to be hand-checked to make sure there are no errors or omissions.

If your RFP consists of questions or fields on a website, creating the shred will be a manual process, but it is still worth doing.

It is tempting to skip over RFP sections and only strip the ones that seem relevant to the proposal. But virtually every sentence in an RFP is there for a reason and merits attention. Even if the statement or phrase is not something to be directly addressed in the proposal and only pertains to the execution of the contract, it still matters during the proposal phase. It could affect the price, the resources required to implement the contract or the level of risk entailed in executing the work.

Some proposal sections will not translate easily into a table format. It will be cumbersome to convert forms, images or spreadsheets. This is addressed in step 8.

Step 2: Add Traceability back to RFP Documents

The next step is to make sure that the lines in the shred are traceable back to the RFP. That means documenting the RFP section that the requirement resides in. If time permits, it is even better to have the RFP paragraph and page number associated with the requirement, but this can be a tedious process, and most RFPs can be searched electronically. The easiest way to document the RFP section is to add a column to the table and populate it with the relevant RFP section or document.

Step 3: Add Columns as Needed to Isolate Different Types of Requirements

Each line in the shred belongs to a specific RFP section. However, RFP section titles can be misleading and not easily understandable to people not familiar with proposal development. For example, the "instruction" heading in an RFP might contain both formatting instructions and information on what content is required for proposal submission. That is why you might have to add a column that provides additional information about the requirement. Depending on the RFP, you might want to be able to isolate requirements that pertain specifically to technical standards, performance measures, product specifications, service level agreements, subcontracting, tasks and subtasks, security, legal, key personnel requirements, certifications, program management, desktop publishing, editing, human resources or pricing. Over time, it helps to develop a standard list of categories, but each RFP is likely to include unique requirements that do not fall neatly into a pre-existing definition.

If the RFP contains multiple documents, add a column to reflect which document contains the requirement. For example, some US government agencies issue a request for quotation (RFQ), similar to an RFP, as one document and a performance work statement (PWS) as a separate document. If you do not associate requirements with specific files, it will be more difficult to find them later on in the RFP if you need to see them in context.

Step 4: Identify Requirements to be Addressed in the Proposal

The next step is to identify and isolate RFP language that describes proposal content as opposed to other information. In the example below, there would be a separate column for this. This is an important part of the analysis for several reasons. In US government RFPs, for example, in addition to technical requirements or specifications, you are likely to also find a lot of RFP text that consists of background information, instructions about proposal format and delivery, assumptions or legal clauses. There

Do These Requirements Have to Be Specifically Addressed in the Proposal?

Disaster Recovery Facility

In the event of a test or actual catastrophic failure, the Government may establish a Government-controlled/Government-owned Disaster Recovery Facility and shall require the Contractor to transition seamlessly to that facility as directed by the Government.

The Government's intention is to initiate the transition to the disaster recovery facility, located within the DC Metropolitan Area, without a disruption of service in accordance with the Continuity of Operations (COOP) procedures.

Travel

All travel shall be conducted in accordance with the Federal Travel Regulation (FTR).

The Contractor shall submit all travel requests to the Contracting Officer's Representative for approval at least two weeks prior to the date the required travel is to begin.

All travel requires advance Government approval/authorization and notification.

Local travel will not be reimbursed.

Local travel is defined as travel within a 50-mile radius of the Government's worksite.

might be information about the operating hours of the customer's building or a requirement that all personnel wear badges inside the building. Not all of these are addressed in every proposal, and, in a page-limited proposal, it might not make sense to use up page count addressing them. On the other hand, maybe the customer has seen a recent increase in security incidents that has raised sensitivity around badges, in which case inserting a paragraph on badging might be the right decision. Doing this now saves time later when you prepare a proposal outline. It will make it easier to allocate pages to different proposal sections and determine how many people will be needed to generate proposal content.

Proposal managers do not always know what is required for the proposal to be considered compliant and what is optional. One rule of thumb for US government RFPs is that, if the statement contains the word "shall," it should be specifically addressed in the proposal. Ultimately, the decision about which requirements should be specifically addressed and allocated space in the proposal is a judgment call. The proposal manager should make an initial determination as to which lines in the shred pertain to proposal content and then ask subject matter experts or legal, contractual or finance staff to review it.

Step 5: Highlight Specific Words That Are Red Flags

The next step is to highlight certain words that could constitute a problem or challenge. The reason people miss important information in the RFP is that they try to read it like a book. Focusing on specific words that are potential red flags is much easier than reading a series of paragraphs. Some of these red flags might cause you to decide to not submit a proposal at all. An RFP might contain requirements or constraints that are too onerous or too risky. For example, certifications and licenses can be expensive to get and maintain. One example is the Federal Information Security Management

Potential Red Flags

- Above
- Adequate
- After
- All
- Always
- Any
- Before
- Below
- Cannot
- Complete
- Each
- Every
- Exclude
- Include
- Inside
- Maximum
- May
- May Not
- Minimum

Act (FISMA) standards required for some systems that support US government agencies. Compliance with FISMA can be time-consuming, expensive or even impossible. For a small business, this requirement alone can result in a no-bid decision. But other requirements might reveal that you have unique advantages or qualifications no one else can meet. A "starter" list quickly expands to include terms that are specific to the industry, the customer or the technology.

- Must
- Never
- No Later Than
- Only
- Outside
- Over
- Penalty
- Shall
- Should
- Sufficient
- Under
- Will

Be sure to apply formatting to these words so that they stand out. You can underline or use yellow highlighting or a different font. This is another way to avoid skipping over potentially critical requirements. You can use an automated tool to find and highlight the words, but you can also do it with most word processing software applications (it will take a bit longer).

Your finished table will be traceable back to a specific RFP or RFQ section, it will have a description (the topic) for each line and it will draw attention to potential red flags as well as proposal content that is required.

Creating this table can involve a substantial investment in time, even with automated tools. It is an investment that will pay off because it results in a checklist that you can use for multiple purposes. It is especially helpful for proposal reviews. A condensed version of the table can be used to check compliance with instructions and responsiveness to requirements. You can delete the topic and RFP document columns, for example, and add a column labeled "compliance" or "responsiveness." The term "compliance matrix" means different things to different organizations, but it is very hard to make sure that your proposal will be considered acceptable without a checklist similar to the one in Table 1.1. The table provides a common format for reviewers to note gaps, inaccuracies and suggested edits.

Step 6: Prepare Instructions and Designate Owners

The next step is to assign owners. Each line in the shred should have one owner; that person is responsible, throughout the entire proposal process, for:

- Determining whether or not to ask a question to clarify the requirement and, if so, developing the question;

Table 1.1

Requirement	*RFP Section*	*Topic*	*Include in Proposal?*	*RFP Document*
Provide an overall management plan that identifies key personnel, the percentage of each person's time that will be committed to the project and describes the functions and responsibilities of each key person relative to the task to be performed	Instruction	Program management	Proposal content	RFP
In addition, the management plan shall describe the experience of all key members	Instruction	Program management	Proposal content	RFP
The Proposer must include a description of the organizational structure and management methodology used to provide service reliability and means of coordination and communication	Instruction	Program management	Proposal content	RFP
The Management Team plan shall identify the various staffing levels, including key managerial and supervisory personnel as well as office location and operational capabilities, for each area of the work as described in the Scope of Services	Instruction	Program management	Proposal content	RFP
It shall clearly describe the functions and responsibilities of each staff member listed and all Subcontractors/Subconsultants and include their experience relative to the tasks to be performed	Instruction	Subcontracting	Proposal content	RFP
Construct the Technical Proposal (using 8½″ × 11″ paper), plus up to four (4) larger foldout pages	Instruction	Desktop publishing	Format instructions	RFP
Use a type size of twelve (12) point or larger Times New Roman font	Instruction	Desktop publishing	Format instructions	RFP
Use margins no less than 1″ at top and ½″ at bottom and sides	Instruction	Desktop publishing	Format instructions	RFP
In the language of the Technical Proposal, do not use ambiguous words such as may, might, should, etc.; use only definite statements of what the Proposer will or will not accomplish	Instruction	Editing	Content instructions	RFP
The entire Technical Proposal is limited to a maximum of 35 total pages, not counting bindings and covers	Instruction	Desktop publishing	Format instructions	RFP
Sequentially number all pages	Instruction	Desktop publishing	Format instructions	RFP
A page with information on both sides is considered two pages	Instruction	Desktop publishing	Format instructions	RFP

(Continued)

Table 1.1 (Continued)

Requirement	*RFP Section*	*Topic*	*Include in Proposal?*	*RFP Document*
It is recognized that existing financial reports, documents, or brochures, such as those that delineate the Proposer's general capabilities and experience, may not comply with the prescribed format	Instruction	Desktop publishing	Format instructions	RFP
It is not the intent to have these documents reformatted and if used, they will be acceptable in their existing form	Instruction	Desktop publishing	Format instructions	RFP
Include all relevant material for each section with the appropriate sections; do not include any appendices, exhibits, resumes, or information in any form outside of the Section appropriate for that information	Instruction	Desktop publishing	Format instructions	RFP
Also provide the Technical Proposal in digital format on a USB drive	Instruction	Desktop publishing	Format instructions	RFP
Acceptable formats include Microsoft Word, Adobe PDF, and HTML	Instruction	Desktop publishing	Format instructions	RFP
Key personnel includes the Service Desk Manager, Program Manager, Request Fulfillment Manager, and a Quality Manager	Special contract requirements	Key personnel	Proposal content	RFP
The Contractor's management team and technical expert staff shall be available for issue-driven meetings called by the Contracting Officer's Representative	PWS	Program management	Proposal content	PWS
For outages, the Contractor shall be available to meet in-person (preferred if capable) or via WebEx within 15 minutes of being notified	PWS	Program management	Proposal content	PWS
For all other inquiries/issues, the Contractor shall be readily available for call/WebEx within 60 minutes	PWS	Program management	Proposal content	PWS
If outages occur outside of business hours, meetings may be required outside the normal business hours	PWS	Program management	Proposal content	PWS
All staff proposed for this task order must be US citizens	PWS	Human resources	Proposal content	RFP
All information generated or provided by this task order shall be protected from unauthorized access, use, disclosure, duplication, modification, diversion, or destruction, whether accidental or intentional, in order to maintain the security, confidentiality, integrity, and availability of such information	RFP	Security	Proposal content	RFP

- Making sure that the solution, methodology or tools are compatible with the requirement;
- Making sure that the requirement is addressed in the proposal or making the determination that it is not necessary to write to it specifically;
- Repeating the first three steps if the RFP requirement changes through revisions or amendments.

You will likely need to consult with the capture manager or senior executive to decide who the owners should be. On large US government proposals, some typical owners are the contract specialists, the pricers, the technical subject matter experts, the human resources department and the proposal production team.

Step 7: Explain Assignment to Owners

Contact each owner, provide the shred and explain which lines that person is responsible for. The owners will need instructions, especially if they do not have experience analyzing RFPs. Tell each expert to read specific lines in the shred and identify, where they exist, the following potential issues: risks, contradictions or inconsistencies, and overly vague or overly specific language.

Risks

Risks or opportunities are often evident when experts see the highlighted words. Any time there is a numerical goal or a superlative such as "always" or "never," it is worth making sure that you can explain how you will meet the requirement in the proposal and then live with it during execution. However, that same superlative can offer a way to distinguish your solution from the other bidders. If a bidder "must" have a certain certification that is hard to get or maintain, and your company has that certification, you will want to use that advantage in the proposal.

For the Solo Practitioner

Follow these same steps. Assign some sections to yourself and, if it is a long solicitation, break the work up into short sessions. Use your network to get help with sections you do not understand. Start with professionals you know and trust and continue to build a team of professional colleagues who can provide expertise in finance, contracts, software or any other area unfamiliar to you.

Contradictions or Inconsistencies

Because many different people contribute to an RFP, sometimes RFPs contain mixed messages. One page might tell you that resumes are included in the page count, and another page might say that they are excluded. One section might have a list of eight key personnel, and the pricing tables might not include the correct lines to bid those people.

Overly Vague or Overly Specific Language

Language that is too vague or too specific could signal a risk during execution, and it could be a signal that the buyer already has a preferred bidder.

A bidder with a lot of knowledge about the customer will know exactly how to interpret vague and general language. A team that is not confident about how to interpret these statements is at a disadvantage and should consider asking questions to clarify and get additional detail. This is another illustration of the principle that the best proposal cannot compensate for a lack of customer knowledge.

Overly specific language can be just as troublesome. Requirements that a vendor have an office in a particular state, city or neighborhood or that the vendor or its personnel have certifications that are difficult or time-consuming to obtain are effective ways of discouraging or shutting out bidders who do not have them. If your team does not pay attention to these now, you might be wasting resources on a bid you cannot win. Document these issues and any notes about how to resolve them (see Table 1.2).

Be sure to tell the owners how to document any risks or issues they uncover and any questions they might want to ask. The easiest way to do this is to add a column to the shred so that everyone is working in a similar

format and files can be easily combined. Give them a due date. For many proposals, the analysis of the RFP has to take place quickly because there is a deadline after which the customer will not answer any more questions.

If you cannot find an owner for some of the lines in the shred, as the proposal manager, you have to own them until you can identify someone. The proposal manager also usually owns all the requirements that pertain to how the proposal should be organized, formatted and delivered and how it will be evaluated. But the proposal manager should also be

Table 1.2

Requirement	*RFP Section*	*Topic*	*Issue*
Develop strategies and design the architecture of the next generation information systems for the program management office	PWS	Technical requirement	Vague: what is the current architecture? What does the customer think the next generation entails?
Develop strategic and innovative solutions to meet enterprise business needs	PWS	Technical requirement	Vague: what kinds of solutions? Hardware? Software? Cloud?
Improve and enhance processes	PWS	Technical requirement	Vague: what type of processes? Software development? Security? Program management? Quality?
Customer satisfaction as measured monthly shall be maintained above 99%	PWS	Service level agreement	Risk: PWS does not say how satisfaction will be measured or by whom
The program manager must have current CISSP, Ethical Hacker, ITIL, Lean Six Sigma and PMP certifications	RFQ	Key personnel requirement	No one person is likely to have this set of certifications
The contractor shall be able to manufacture 350 XYS cables per hour and scale up to more than 700 per hour when required	PWS	Service level agreement	We have never been able to produce more than 150 an hour
The contractor shall maintain a program management office in Wiseman, Alaska	PWS	Management requirement	The program management office required has a staff of 12; how will we find people who are willing to move there?

as familiar as possible with the entire RFP, including all the attachments, spreadsheets and appendices, and able to answer any questions. You do not have to understand all the technical details. But you should have an understanding of what the different sections or documents contain and how they relate to each other.

Step 8: Capture and Assign RFP Charts, Illustrations and so on That Are Not in the Shred

The next step is to go through all the RFP sections that you were not able to capture in the shred. These usually include spreadsheets, charts, graphics, illustrations, manuals, regulations and photographs. Assign an owner to each one. Do not skip this step. I have seen proposal teams prepare pricing using their own proprietary pricing tables until the day before the proposal was due, only to find out that the customer-provided spreadsheet had locked cells and corrupt formulas. Open every file and scrutinize every item that is too cumbersome to include in the shred.

Step 9: Convene and Conduct an RFP Meeting

The next step is to conduct a meeting at which each expert presents RFP risks, contradictions, overly vague or specific language, and any other concerns. Each participant should show up with a shred that shows the issues discovered. If you do not have the authority or credibility to make this request, find a senior executive who will support you. Gathering the experts together to report on each section of the RFP has three advantages. First, requiring a formal presentation creates accountability. Second, the deliverables for the meeting create an audit trail in case someone new joins the team or there is a delay. Third, the meeting gives everyone a chance to learn about parts of the RFP they do not understand. Because you are giving them the RFP in a digestible form, you have reduced their workload, and their eye-strain.

The main purpose of a meeting to discuss the RFP is the development of a list of questions or issues. Most competitive RFPs offer the bidders the opportunity to ask questions about the RFP for a limited period of time after it is released. This is because even sophisticated customers make mistakes when they issue RFPs, and a question period provides the opportunity to clear up misunderstandings. This is helpful to the buyer as well as the bidders, but the window for asking questions can be very short. This is one reason that analysis of the RFP is the first of my fundamentals and occurs early in the process. If the RFP does not contain instructions for asking questions, contact the customer to find out how to pose questions.

Step 10: Develop and Edit Questions

If you have followed the steps above, you will have probably already developed a list of potential concerns. Evaluate each one to see if it merits being turned into a formal question for the customer. Questions are often visible to the other bidders; asking a question can reveal knowledge that other bidders do not have and take away a competitive advantage. If your RFP includes vague language, and you know how to interpret it, it might not be to your advantage to ask for clarification. On the other hand, it is important to question contradictions or inconsistencies that affect compliance with the requirements, such as an instruction to submit a paper copy on one page and an instruction to submit an electronic copy on another page.

Think about the implications of the answers to your questions and plan for the worst case. For example, if the instructions do not indicate whether resumes are included in the page count, assume that they are. It is much easier to do that than to cut large amounts of text at the last minute. If the RFP implies, but does not say, that bidders have to hold certain certifications, assume that those certifications will be mandatory until you learn otherwise.

Do not ask a question if you run the risk of getting an answer that would put you at a disadvantage or even cause your company to decide not to bid. If the RFP is silent on an issue, and you can submit a compliant proposal without getting clarification, it is often a good idea to refrain from asking the question. For example, the RFP might include a statement such as "Only the required key personnel are permitted to deliver the oral presentation." It is not clear if the buyer expects **all** the required key personnel at the presentation, or if the intent is to **exclude non-key** personnel. So, if one of your key people cannot be present at the oral presentation, do not ask which interpretation is correct.

Agree on what your assumptions will be if the customer does not answer your questions, because often the answers arrive late in the proposal process. Sometimes the answers are even more ambiguous than the original proposal text. Delaying the solution development, outline, writing or reviewing until you get a clear answer can mean insufficient time to finish the proposal before the deadline.

Refrain from annoying the buyer by asking a question about a requirement that contains an obvious clerical error unless it raises serious compliance questions. Everyone makes mistakes. You will not get extra points for showing that you are smarter than the person who wrote the RFP. If there are pages or sections missing, however, since you do not know what might be on those pages, it is important to ask whether or not it was an oversight.

Even if you elect to not submit a question on a particular requirement, discuss it and agree as a team how to address it. Then, document your decision. The ticking clock is the biggest challenge during the competitive proposal process. If different people on the proposal team start to write sections, create graphics, populate pricing templates or engage teammates and subcontractors with differing ideas of what a particular word or phrase means, it wastes valuable time. Differing interpretations of customer-specific terms within the proposal team can result in price estimates that do not align with the solution, staffing charts that do not align with the price and significant reworkings and revisions. If the differing interpretations are discovered late in the process, it is not always possible to recover.

Exactly how to phrase questions is an art form, and it can change depending on the type of solicitation and the level of customer knowledge. The wording and even the formatting can make a significant difference in the answer you receive, and the answer you receive can change your proposal dramatically, as seen in Table 1.3.

Step 11: Document Questions, Assumptions and Answers

The final step is to agree on the wording of the questions and submit them before the deadline. After submittal, as proposal manager, you should post them, along with the questions you did not ask and all your assumptions, somewhere everyone on the team has access to them. Otherwise, people will waste time rummaging through their inbox when they cannot

Table 1.3

Rule	*Example*
Number the questions	
Keep questions short	Instead of: "1. All bidders have multiple documents to prepare on a very compressed schedule and there is no way of knowing what might have been included in missing sections and attachments. This represents a challenge to finishing the bid on time and submitting a compelling proposal, especially given all the specific security requirements. It would be helpful to get Attachments 9 and 10 as soon as possible." Ask: "1. Will the government please provide bidders with Attachments 9 and 10 as soon as possible?"
Include the specific language from the RFP, as well as the RFP page and section number	"2. PWS section 4.7.2 on page 84 says 'All equipment proposed for incorporation in the system must be manufactured in the continental United States.' Does this preclude using equipment from US manufacturers whose parent companies are not US corporations?"

(*Continued*)

Table 1.3 (Continued)

Rule	*Example*
Make sure you are asking a question and not telling the customer what to do	Instead of: "3. Provide pages missing from Attachment 7." Ask: "3. Would the government please provide pages 7 and 8 that appear to be missing from Attachment 7?"
Ask questions that can be answered with a "yes" or "no"	"4 Are bidders permitted to hand-deliver proposals?"
Avoid either/or questions, because you might get back a yes or no answer which will not resolve the issue. Separate out the two options and ask a question about each one	Instead of: "5. Do the penalties for late deliverables affect the prime contractor only or the subcontractors as well?" Ask: "5. Do the penalties for late deliverables affect the prime contractor?" And "6. Do the penalties for late delivery flow down to the subcontractors?"
Do not bundle questions together	Instead of: "7. Is it acceptable to submit the proposal electronically and what formats are acceptable?" Ask: "7. Is it acceptable to submit the proposal electronically?" And "8. What electronic formats are acceptable?"
Suggest the answer that you want to receive back from the government in the body of your question and add any specifics that will provide clarity	Instead of: "9. What type of delivery will be accepted?" Ask: "9. Will the government accept email delivery of the proposal to the contracting officer?"
When appropriate, provide the reason for your question	"10. Due to the impending hurricane and the unreliability of commercial courier services, will the government accept email delivery of the proposal to the contracting officer instead of physical delivery of the proposal on a DVD?"
Explain why it is in the customer's best interest to answer the question in a certain way	Instead of: "11. Will the government provide separate columns in the spreadsheet for each year of the contract?" Ask: "11. In order for the government to be able to better compare solutions and prices across different proposals, would the government provide separate columns in the spreadsheet for each year of the contract?"

remember how to interpret a word or phrase. The assumptions and submitted questions should become your baseline list that you update when you receive answers to questions. Sometimes there are multiple rounds of questions and answers, because answers can contain their own ambiguities and inconsistencies. Each time you receive answers to questions, including answers to questions asked by other bidders, update the list. Keeping the documentation current and accurate is essential, because you might not receive a revised RFP that reflects answers to questions.

Conclusion: Scaling the Process

This is, admittedly, a long and perhaps overly detailed process to squeeze into the short time frame between when the RFP is released and when questions are due. Sometimes that window is only a few days. RFPs can contain multiple documents and hundreds of pages. It is hard to get the time and attention of the experts. Shredding and formatting the shred take time, and no one wants another meeting added to the calendar.

The reality is that you might not be able to execute all the steps early in the process for every document of every RFP. So, if you cannot follow all the steps described here, do as many as you can. If you cannot search for all the potential red flags, search for as many as you can. If you cannot fully format a shred, at least create a shred. If you cannot convene all the experts for an RFP meeting, conduct a meeting with anyone who can participate, even if it is only you and one other person. Almost any activity you can do will put you ahead of the team that tries to manage the process by using the RFP documentation as it is published. The more steps you can follow, the sooner, the more time and trouble you can save down the road.

Notes

1 Keith Rayner, Alexander Pollatsek, Jane Ashby, and Charles Clifton Jr., *The Psychology of Reading*, Psychology Press, 2011; Trevor A. Harley, *The Psychology of Language: From Data to Theory*, 4th Edition, Psychology Press, 2013; Keith Rayner, Lester C. Loschky, and Eyal M. Reingold, "Eye movements in visual cognition: The contributions of George W. McConkie," *Visual Cognition*, 2014, Vol. 22, Nos. 3–4, 239–241, http://dx.doi.org/10.1080/13506285.2014.895463; Michael A. Arbib, "Schema-theoretic models of arm, hand and eye movements," *Neuroscience: From Neural Networks to Artificial Intelligence*, 1993, Vol. 4.

2 https://www.freelancewriting.com/copywriting/proofreading-exercise/.

Chapter 2

Solution Development and Definition

Definition

The term "solution" appears most frequently in descriptions of the process for bidding on US federal government contracts. However, the concept applies to all proposals. In its simplest form, the solution is what is being offered to the customer. This could mean people, hardware, systems, software, real estate, products, utilities (power, bandwidth), financial instruments or some combination of these. Solution definition is the process of clarifying exactly what is being offered and making sure everyone involved in the proposal has the same understanding of the product or service. If you are applying for a research grant, the solution consists of the people on your team, the data you will collect, the methodology you will use, the types of conclusions you will reach and the ways in which the research results will be applied. Defining the solution is rarely a cut-and-dried process and it often requires multiple iterations, especially if the RFP undergoes modifications. The term "solution" can be ambiguous for beginning and even advanced proposal managers. Proposal management literature has many references to "the solution" as though the meaning of the term will be immediately understood.

Developing the solution entails collecting detailed information, interpreting language from the RFP and documenting decisions. Also, creating drawings, charts, text and calculations that fully explain the details of what you are offering. Whereas the purpose of the proposal is to convince the customer to select your company, the first goal of solution definition is to make sure that your product or service will meet the customer's needs after the contract is awarded. It makes little sense to invest time and energy in a proposal for a solution that will not work or meet the customer's requirements. Because of this, there might be a lot of solution-related information that never gets incorporated into the proposal; it is nevertheless important to work through the details so that you will be able to price competitively and execute successfully after the contract is awarded.

DOI: 10.4324/9781003581475-3

Defining the solution can take five minutes on a laptop with only one person involved or it can entail a series of meetings with multiple subject matter experts over days, weeks, months or longer. It depends on the content of the RFP, the size of the organization, the complexity of the bid and the number of people in the organization who have to be consulted.

Why Is it Important?

The solution is often the factor that determines who will win a competitive contract, and a description of the solution, even if not comprehensive, is almost always a required component of the proposal. A well-articulated solution can outweigh other evaluation factors and offset a higher price or other perceived flaws in the proposal. Developing the solution is a prerequisite for determining a competitive price. The solution is also an important planning document because it describes the resources (people, hardware, infrastructure) your organization will need to execute the contract after award.

The reason that this book devotes an entire chapter to solution development is the frequency with which even seasoned professionals skip this step. Here is a hypothetical sequence of events (Table 2.1), analogous to

Table 2.1 Typical Solution Development Timetable

Time	*Event*
March 2023	The section owners began writing proposal content based on a draft RFP
April–May 2023	The proposal manager organized several reviews, and the team received many comments on the proposal draft
June–August 2023	The owners addressed the comments and revised the document
September 12, 2023	The final RFP was released with a 21-day deadline
September 19, 2023	The capture manager engaged additional reviewers who were subject matter experts. They provided comments such as the following: "The program manager should have at least five years of cloud implementation experience to be a compelling candidate for the position." "The transition process proposed will take three months longer than what is in the proposal due to the time it takes to get clearances processed." "The method for escalating from Tier 1 to Tier 2 is not realistic given the staffing profile."

(*Continued*)

Table 2.1 (Continued)

Time	*Event*
September 22, 2023	The engineers and subject matter experts met to address the comments and created a new plan for the solution
September 23, 2023	The proposal manager met with the team to explain that the new proposal content had to be finished within a week to allow enough time for pricing, editing, formatting and delivery. In the end, the team decided not to bid at all since there was not time to prepare a compelling proposal

one in my own recent experience, that shows what happens when there is no clear solution definition before the team begins to generate proposal content.

Re-engineering is not the only risk. If the proposal manager, the writers, the pricing experts and the contract and legal professionals do not share an understanding of what you are proposing, everyone does their job in a vacuum. Some writers know what the solution should be, others believe they know but are wrong, and others do not know and resort to what proposal managers refer to as MSU (making stuff up). The result is that different components of the proposal (technical approach, past performance, resumes, company qualifications, staffing) are likely to contradict each other, requiring many cycles of revision and reworking. Or the writers fail to complete writing assignments on time, not out of laziness but because they lack information. Deadlines slip. Although it might take time to align everyone at the beginning, it will take much more time, often time that does not exist, to get everyone on the same page midway through the proposal or (even worse) at the very end.

Challenges

The explanation as to why the solution matters shows that the proposal manager cannot fulfill essential functions of the job such as reviews, proofreading, editing, production and schedule management if the solution is undefined or constantly changing. Yet, often, proposal teams do not appreciate the value of spending the necessary time and energy to develop and document the solution. It is common for proposal teams to skip this step and assign each section of the proposal to a knowledgeable and experienced writer, assuming that the solution will be created through the process of writing, especially when the RFP response time is short. They invent the solution as they are writing the proposal.

The converse can also occur. Dedicated solution teams can take on a life of their own, go off on tangents and develop solutions that are not practical or are outside the budget constraints. It is then difficult to get the team to refocus.

A related challenge is the inclination of some subject matter experts and business development managers to create a solution they think the customer should want instead of what is asked for in the RFP. The RFP represents the culmination of a sales cycle, sometimes a long sales cycle. Before the RFP is published, buyers (government and commercial) spend time planning, doing research, talking to potential vendors, explaining their objectives and gathering information. Over time, they refine and sometimes change their ideas. Likewise, business development professionals collect information about the buying history of the customer, about perceived likes and dislikes, about personnel changes and about the likely competitors for a particular opportunity. All this information is relevant and important when developing the solution and proposal content because it provides context. Responding to a solicitation in a vacuum, without this context, is the equivalent of shooting in the dark.

However, the information collected by the business development team might not be in alignment with the content of the RFP. Over time, stakeholders in the customer's organization compromise and even change their mind. The individuals in control of the purse strings might not see the value of sophisticated technical features. What emerges is a consensus document that might not resemble information collected by potential bidders before the solicitation is issued.

A typical scenario is one where a company's sales or marketing team meets regularly with one set of stakeholders in the customer's organization. Often, it is the end users who will actually benefit from enhanced features or the latest technology and they are often the people who are the least sensitive to budget constraints. As the months go by, the sales team continues to talk to end users and often does not (sometimes, cannot) talk to the customer stakeholders who make the economic decisions. The team becomes more and more convinced that their solution is exactly what the customer is looking for. The longer the process lasts, the more confident the sales team is of the customer's preference. Then, the RFP is released and it calls for a less sophisticated, and less costly, approach.

In a competitive environment, the buyers have to make decisions based on what is in the RFP. Otherwise, it would defeat the purpose of having a competition in the first place. For US government acquisitions, the contracting officers are required by law to award contracts based on what is in the RFP and can face significant penalties, some of them criminal, if they are found to have violated the law. Therefore, it is wise to be cautious about using information that has been obtained unofficially. For most competitive acquisitions, the RFP trumps all other sources of information. If, for example, the RFP calls for a help desk that is manned 12 hours a day, and the salesperson is absolutely confident that the customer wants a helpdesk that is manned 24 hours a day, the smart bidder will propose one that is manned 12 hours a day (and perhaps offer additional, optional pricing for the other 12 hours, if the RFP permits that type of pricing).

When Does it Happen?

Documenting the solution typically follows the detailed analysis of the RFP. But this is not the best approach. The moment your company decides to pursue an opportunity, that is the moment that solution definition should begin, even if it means proceeding with incomplete information. The process can be long and iterative. Regardless of whether it begins before or after RFP release, solution definition always precedes creation of proposal text or graphics. Otherwise, you run the risk of expensive and time-consuming revisions.

Who Owns it?

This activity differs from some of the proposal management responsibilities discussed in other chapters because of the role of the proposal manager. The other chapters describe activities that the proposal manager can influence and direct, if not control. Although the proposal manager is accountable for making sure the solution is developed, defined, documented and communicated, those tasks are the responsibility of other professionals: engineers, subject matter experts, managers, senior leadership. If no one has this responsibility when you join the proposal team, ask that someone be assigned to it as soon as possible. If the capture manager or senior executive tells you that the solution has already been documented, ask to see it and make sure that whoever prepared it addressed the activities in steps two through seven below. If the solution has not been fully developed, the proposal manager can provide support by tracking progress, and facilitating and documenting details and assumptions.

Sometimes, perhaps often, the solution is too technical for a proposal manager to fully understand. Some research projects involve theoretical concepts and models whose descriptions appear to be written in a different language altogether. So, it is not surprising that many proposal managers do not even try to facilitate or support; they leave the solution to engineers and other subject matter experts or executives. Often, the schedule makes it difficult to engage in solution meetings and activities.

But the more a proposal manager can learn about the solution, the more effective that manager will be. Knowledge about the solution will help the proposal manager create and stick to a realistic schedule. It will also make it possible to more effectively coach writers and other contributors as to how to improve proposal text, graphics, charts or tables. Furthermore, leaving the process entirely to others carries significant risks. The solution is at the core of the proposal and interdependent with many other proposal sections. It is very difficult for a proposal manager who does not understand anything about the solution and does not track solution-related activities to keep the proposal on schedule and deliver it on time.

Steps in the Process

The activities described here are the typical ones that the solution architect or solution team execute, in chronological order, with support and structure from the proposal manager as appropriate. In practice, solution definition is often iterative, and some organizations have their own specific methodologies and processes. Some proposal managers are involved in all solution activities and help to drive important decisions.

Others participate episodically as observers. Some proposal managers are completely hands-off and just track progress through meetings with the solution architect. In a perfect world, more involvement is better. But, regardless of how involved the proposal manager is in the development of the solution, the proposal manager should, jointly with the business development manager or senior executive, establish a schedule for completing the solution development and documentation. It is easy for a team of subject matter experts to lose sight of the fact that the rest of the proposal is effectively on hold until the solution development is complete. The solution phase can turn into a "science project" unless you have a way for all the experts involved to come to agreement within a defined time frame.

In supporting the solution team, proposal managers should be aware of solution traps that can result in lengthy debates and then resurface if

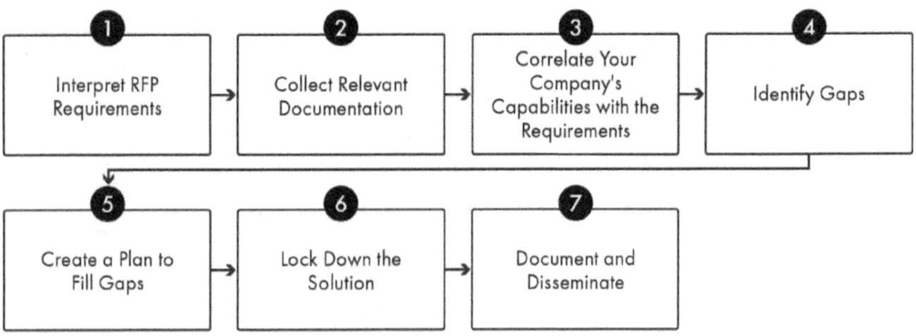

Figure 2.1 Solution Development Process

they are not resolved. These include overly vague language in the RFP, multiple offerings that all meet the customer's requirements, and implied requirements gleaned from customer contact or experience working in the customer's organization. For each one, the proposal manager should encourage the solution team to reach a decision and then agree to cut off debate unless there is new information.

Vague RFP Language

A thorough understanding of RFP requirements requires subject matter expertise, especially when the RFP language is open to interpretation. Solution teams often find that requirements that initially appear straightforward during early analysis of the RFP become less clear, as in the example in Table 2.2.

As discussed in Chapter 1, the time to identify overly specific or overly vague terminology is during the analysis of the RFP and the development of questions. But, if the customer does not answer the question or if you decide, for competitive reasons, to not ask the question, during the solution development process someone must decide what "optimal" and "ergonomic" mean here. Typically, the person who knows the customer the best and has the most experience with that particular offering is the one who should make the final interpretation. For more complicated RFPs, you will have to consult subject matter experts as well as sales and marketing staff. Whoever makes the decision, it is important to make it early, make it definitive and document it. Otherwise, late in the process, when there is no more time, someone is likely to revisit the unclear language and suggest a different solution or interpretation. This is where many proposal teams encounter last-minute panic and introduce errors into the proposal.

Choosing Models, Processes or Technologies

Even with requirements that are not ambiguous, solution teams often have to make decisions about which product or service is best. If several models

Table 2.2

Requirement	*Ambiguity*
The system will have **optimal** flight modes for indoor flight but will also be capable of outdoor flight	Who is defining optimal, and how?
The GCS should be compact and **ergonomically** designed	Is there a particular ergonomic standard or feature that is needed?

or methodologies or approaches satisfy the requirement, which is the best one to offer? Do you want to focus on lower cost, improved performance, reliability or additional features?

Implied or Hidden Requirements

Solution teams often debate hidden or implied requirements. People familiar with customer preferences often want to address and include features they believe the customer wants that are not stated explicitly. They might see a discrepancy between what they know, or what they think they know, and the requirements as expressed in the RFP, and they cannot understand why certain requirements were excluded. Or they might see a contradiction between what they learned before the RFP was released and what appeared in the final RFP itself. In other situations, the team has no

"I know what they really want ... and it is not what is in the RFP! We should propose the RIGHT solution instead!"

knowledge other than what is in the RFP and has to guess about what is implied or excluded.

Addressing these implied or hidden requirements and including them in the solution can constitute a strength and set you apart from the competition. However, this can also add to the price and the risk, and they might be seen as a distraction by the evaluators. They take time away from answering the requirements that are mandatory. Most buyers have to follow strict rules and cannot make a judgment based on features that were not specifically requested in the RFP. Reliable knowledge about the customer's likes, dislikes and buying history is the only way to make an informed judgment in each situation.

A requirement for professional services might include a requirement such as "Provide personnel who possess the necessary skills, abilities, and credentials to perform services of a pharmacist and a current license to practice pharmacy in the State of Colorado." Perhaps your team can propose a pharmacist who meets all the requirements and is also a registered nurse with clinical experience. The salary and the cost to the customer might be higher, but the pharmacist would be able to complete certain tasks more efficiently and deliver better services. Would the customer see this? The answer depends entirely on whether the customer will appreciate the faster service. Encourage the subject matter experts and others involved to consider implied requirements and address them, as long as everyone labels them "implied" or "inferred" rather than explicit.

Step 1: Interpretation of RFP Requirements

The person who owns the solution, often referred to in the government proposal world as the solution architect, must be familiar with the details of the product or service specified in the RFP, as well as any conditions or quality standards that have to be met. The proposal manager can help by creating a list of everything in the RFP that pertains to the product or service the customer is buying. These reflect the needs of the people who will actually use the product or service. Government solicitations typically include a section called "Statement of Work" or "Performance Work Statement" that lists characteristics, attributes or specifications. But requirements can be buried in RFP sections where you do not expect them. Do not confuse solution requirements with instructions for preparing the proposal, such as page limits or the organization of the proposal document. The performance work statement and the instructions are often written by different people and they do not always align with each other (see Chapter 3).

Some examples of the types of requirements typically found in an RFP are shown in Table 2.3.

Table 2.3

Solution Type	*Requirement Types*	*Sample Requirement*
Services	Personnel requirements Tasks Location Schedule Quality measures	"Train Tier One help desk personnel so that they resolve tickets within five minutes" "Provide personnel who possess the necessary skills, abilities, and credentials to perform services of a pharmacist and a current license to practice pharmacy in the State of Colorado" "Provide qualified personnel staggered to cover all work shifts 24/7, including holidays"
Equipment	Technical specifications Quantity Delivery channel Speed of delivery	"8 PIR Motion Detectors 60 ft with Popit" "12 PIR Motion Sensors 80 ft" "15 Video Xper Flex Servers"
Software	Brand Features Functions Quantity	"Provide for up to 38 users, GNAT Pro Enterprise Ada for x86-64 Windows (64 bits) native, GNAT coverage for x86-64 Windows (64 bits) native, GtkAda for x86-64 Windows (64 bits) native, and CodePeer for 64 bit"
Utilities	Technical specifications Volume Delivery channel	"Jitter should be below 30 ms" "Packet loss should not be more than 1%" "Network latency should not go over 150 ms" "RTT should not exceed 300 ms"

Step 2: Collection of Relevant Documentation

The proposal manager can also support the solution team by collecting existing documentation about relevant products or services you have sold or proposed in the past. These could be reports, briefings, flow charts, job instructions, resumes, specification sheets, white papers, brochures or past proposals. Collect model numbers, names of people, methodologies, tools, databases, facilities, processes and software licenses. This step is even more critical when the proposal team includes people with both long and short tenures with the company – the old-timers take it for granted that everyone else knows as much as they do about products and services. If you are writing a proposal for a research project, look at descriptions of previous, similar projects that were successful in receiving funding.

Check the date to see when the material was prepared and make notes about what has changed in the interim. Companies that have centralized repositories for information about products and services can act much more quickly during the proposal process and have a competitive advantage.

Step 3: Correlation of Your Company's Capabilities with the Requirements

The solution team should line up your existing solution with the specific requirements of the RFP. The simplest way to accomplish this is to add a column to a requirements table you have already created where you identify the details of your product or service and compare those features with the RFP requirements. A requirements table for a product with detailed specifications might look like Table 2.4.

Table 2.4

RFP Requirement	*ABC Company Systems*
The system, utilizing the quadcopter concept, has to be small enough that it can fly through a standard residential door frame (36″)	We tested all our models, and they all fit through a 36″ door frame
The size of the quadcopter is not to exceed 10″ × 10″ and not to exceed a diagonal distance of 14″	Only our STXHG4700 and 4800 models fit the size specification
The system will have optimal flight modes for indoor flight but will also be capable of outdoor flight	All our systems have indoor and outdoor flight modes
Position holding while indoors shall be accomplished without the use of a GPS	All our systems are GPS-dependent but can easily be converted to doppler/RF navigation
Command and control signals shall be AES256 encrypted	All our systems use a different encryption method, but characteristics are the same as those stipulated in AES256
The system shall have the ability to add or remove payloads via a "plug-n-play" method	All our systems have this feature

(Continued)

Table 2.4 (Continued)

RFP Requirement	*ABC Company Systems*
The system shall have a built-in microphone for listening in the ambient environment	None of our models have built-in microphones
The system will have the capability to right itself should it become inverted	We have never tested inversion inside
The system will only require one person to operate, and will operate independent of any smartphone, tablet or "App." Operation will be accomplished via a hand-held controller, called a Ground Control Station (GCS), which will also contain a viewing screen, which is a minimum of 4.75″ wide	All our systems operate independently of apps, tablets or smartphones
The GCS should be compact and ergonomically designed	We took ergonomics into account when designing all our systems
This GCS will not be cellular network-dependent	None of our systems are dependent on a cellular network

Often, the proposal manager does not have the technical expertise needed to complete the solution column. But, often, the proposal manager can start the process and help the subject matter experts by providing structure, facilitating meetings and capturing details.

If the RFP calls for a product with detailed requirements, such as the one above, documenting the existing solution is a straightforward process, although there are almost always judgment calls to be made. When services are involved, documenting the solution entails explaining a process, methodology or approach, and populating a table like the one above can be more challenging. Requirements for services are often expressed as verbs: "train," "manage," "respond," "resolve," "ensure," "implement," "maintain.".

For these requirements, describing the solution usually means defining the steps in the process and sometimes the rationale for the steps and the degree of compliance with industry standards. Steps might be sequential, or they might be logically organized into groups of tasks, according to their function. Table 2.5 is an example of a solution definition for a requirement to monitor the quality of people answering calls at a first tier help desk.

Table 2.5

RFP Requirement	*ABC Company Approach*
The contractor shall implement a quality monitoring process to meet the service level agreements as described in Attachment 1	1. Spot Checking. We already do this. Supervisors are co-located with help desk technicians and walk the floor regularly so that they can spot check by listening to entire calls or portions of calls. (We do this now on all our help desk contracts) 2. Issue Identification. We do not have a standard process for issue identification because the supervisors address them in real time 3. Issue Communication. We already do this. Supervisors communicate with the technician immediately after any call where there is an issue, coach the technician and continue the conversation until there is a shared understanding as to the plan for resolution 4. Issue Documentation. We do not have a standard form that supervisors use to document issues or a way to track issues over time to see trends
The contractor shall report quality metrics for tier one weekly	Our standard process addresses all the requirements: 1. Technician Documentation. Each technician is required to open a ticket at the beginning of the call. Supervisors review tickets at the end of each day to spot any anomalies 2. Report Generation. All tickets are stored in our proprietary InfoTech system, which we configure to generate reports on the quality metrics in Attachment 1 3. Report Delivery. The program manager reviews the InfoTech report each Friday before transmitting to the contracting officer's representative via email
The contractor shall deliver a quality control plan within two weeks of contract award	1. A table of contents of our QC plan is in the proposal 2. A draft will be ready at contract award 3. We will solicit feedback from the COR after award 4. We will incorporate revisions and deliver within a week of contract award

Table 2.6

Requirement	*ABC Company Process/ Approach*	*Competitive Landscape*
The contractor shall report quality metrics for tier one weekly	1. Technician Documentation. Each technician is required to open a ticket at the beginning of the call. Supervisors review tickets at the end of each day to spot any anomalies 2. Report Generation. All tickets are stored in our proprietary InfoTech system which we configure to generate reports on the quality metrics in Attachment 1 3. Report Delivery. The program manager reviews the InfoTech report each Friday before transmitting to the contracting officer's representative via email	The incumbent's system for storing tickets is web-based, whereas ours is not
The system shall have the ability to add or remove payloads via a "plug-n-play" method	Our systems all have this feature	We were the first to market with this feature, and only one other company can offer it

When you have available information about the competition or the marketplace, it is helpful to annotate the table. For example, is an approach or technology new and untested in the marketplace? Is your company the only one who can deliver a certain product? Using the examples in Table 2.4, has some data points that are worth documenting at this stage.

Step 4: Identify Gaps

The solution architect should assess the number of gaps you have between your existing solution and the requirements and their significance. If your business development and marketing teams have been able to influence the requirements in advance of the RFP, your products or services might line up exactly with the requirements. But this is rare. At the other end of the spectrum, you might not meet any of the specifications; this usually leads to a decision to not submit a bid because the likelihood of winning is too low. Most proposal managers encounter a scenario that is in between the two extremes, in which the organization has a product or service that meets some of the requirements, but not all. Document where there are gaps and assess the possibility of closing them. The tailoring of your existing product or service can be quick and mechanical at one end of the spectrum, or highly complex and time-consuming at the other. In the example above, one difference between what the company can do now and what is required is a change in the encryption method. Decoupling the tablet and the GPS system, changing the encryption method and testing to see if the system can fit inside a residential door frame.

Step 5: Create a Plan to Fill Gaps

Filling the gaps between your existing solution and the RFP requirements might be as simple as a minor modification to a product or as complex as building and standing up a new manufacturing plant. Where the gaps are significant, addressing them might require experts from different fields to collaborate. It might require teams dedicated to specific groups of requirements who work simultaneously. Either way, this step typically entails multiple meetings of experts to review and assess options and reach a decision on the best approach.

Although the proposal manager might not contribute to this task in a substantive way, it is important to at least observe these solution sessions and make sure that they remain focused. The proposal manager can add value to the solution process by suggesting methods for facilitating solution meetings or performing the facilitation function. A proposal manager who understands the solution well enough to be able to explain its main features is likely to be more effective in managing the schedule and ensuring compliance with the RFP than one who only engages in the process of preparing the proposal document itself.

Many facilitation techniques can be helpful in achieving consensus on the solution. The key to success is having all the stakeholders in the room at the same time and making sure the discussion has focus and results. Professional facilitation can save hours of time and avoid confusion and conflict later in the process. The term "brainstorming" is often used to describe an unfocused conversation that allows everyone to express a viewpoint and achieve consensus. Practiced by a professional facilitator, the process can be extremely effective. Brainstorming as I have seen it practiced more often consists of an open-ended discussion of different ideas with no conclusions or decisions at the end of the session. Group discussions about the product or service should engage people who have been talking to the customer (salespeople, business development staff and contracts departments, for example). Their knowledge is critical, especially for RFPs that contain vague language or terms that could have multiple meanings. Mind-mapping, Gamestorming, ideation and systems thinking can all help teams reach consensus on technical questions.[1]

Many companies use a process referred to as storyboarding, a term that originated in the movie industry, to document solutions. A storyboard is a paper or electronic document of one to two pages that represents one component of the product or one task or subtask in a service contract. It typically includes an illustration or chart, any dependencies or risks, the relevant RFP requirement, any subcontractor or vendor information, and the associated price or level of effort. Storyboards force the team to think through all the details of the solution, but they can be very time-consuming to populate, especially for short proposals with tight deadlines.

Typically, creating a new solution requires technical expertise, knowledge of the customer's buying patterns and budget, financial information and legal or contractual expertise. The more diverse the solution team, the longer it takes to build the solution. For this reason, as seen in the quadcopter example, it is critical to get as much information as possible on specifications and requirements and begin to design the solution well in advance of the RFP release. Some buyers will publish draft requirements, and, in some instances, the previous contract or RFP is available. If not, it is the responsibility of the sales or business development team to find out as much as possible about the requirements. Waiting until the RFP is released means that there will be limited time for filling gaps.

Solution teams might decide to close the gap by teaming with vendors or subcontractors and outsourcing part of the solution. The tailoring process typically involves a "make versus buy" tradeoff. In some situations, you can close gaps by training people or modifying existing hardware or software ("make"). But, often, the only way a company can respond to a solicitation is to incorporate products and services from another company ("buy"). The "buy" approach offers distinct advantages. For many US government acquisitions, bidders are required to propose the use of vendors and subcontractors that fall into certain categories (small businesses, minority or women-owned businesses, veteran-owned businesses, companies in HUBZones or businesses owned by disabled people). Using disadvantaged businesses can even earn the bidder extras points in the evaluation. Using vendors in these categories can earn the bidder extra points and lower the price. But the buy approach also has drawbacks. It often lowers the profit. The lead time for incorporating external products and services into the proposal is long. It takes time to get product descriptions and price quotes from subcontractors, and some subcontractors have approval chains within their own organizations that can take days or weeks.

Terminology often differs across companies. A request from a subcontractor to send corporate qualifications could mean either a brochure or a lengthy technical document. Agreements between companies often require iterative negotiations; the time involved and administrative burdens entailed can be significant. For this reason, many companies go back to the same subcontractors and vendors; contracts are already negotiated, and many of the players already know each other. Whichever route you choose, the earlier you resolve the make-versus-buy debate, the easier it will be to secure the products and services that are missing from the solution in time to incorporate them successfully.

Some gaps are easy to fill through a make-or-buy analysis and decision. But, if existing products or services do not meet many RFP requirements, and it is not possible to partner with vendors or subcontractors, the team has to build an entirely new solution. Proposal timelines are usually short, and there is rarely time during a competitive proposal to create something entirely new from whole cloth or to make extensive modifications to an existing product or service. At this point, it might be advisable to not submit a proposal at all. Thus, the solution process forces the team to rethink what might have been an ill-informed decision earlier on and cut losses early rather than continuing to invest in a bid that does not make good business sense.

Likewise, if your organization has no documentation about existing products or services that meet any of the requirements of the solicitation, this is a red flag. Proposal managers are rarely in a position to tell senior executives to not bid. However, proposal managers can both raise questions about how long it will take to fill gaps and document the resources that will be required to create an entirely new solution or make significant modifications to an existing product or service. Costs can be expressed as time, opportunity and dollars.

Step 6: Lock Down the Solution

The proposal manager should collaborate with the capture manager, business development manager or another senior executive to bring solution development and definition to closure. If the team continues to debate the solution, it makes it difficult to agree on a final price, to choose the right people to bid and to create the text and graphics for the proposal. Proposal managers do not approve solutions and they often do not know what the organizational approval chain is or how long it takes. It helps to have relationships with people at multiple levels within your company so that you can get information and plan for the approval process. Identify early on who will make the final decision about the solution. It might be a department head, a product manager, an engineer or a senior executive.

Sometimes, multiple approvals are required. In a small organization, the source of authority might be obvious. In a large bureaucracy, degrees of authority can be vague and they can change over time. People over- and underrepresent their ability to make a decision, and responsibilities can change during the course of the proposal if the RFP is revised or if the customer answers questions about RFP requirements. For example, if an early analysis of an RFP suggests that the bid will be $5 million, but answers to questions reveal that the customer has a $20 million budget, the person with the authority to sign off on the solution might change. If the price of the bid is above a given threshold, the decision might be the responsibility of someone high up in the bureaucracy with little knowledge of the customer's requirements and buying history. This means adding time to the proposal schedule to educate whoever is responsible for the final decision.

Once you have the required approvals, work with the solution architect to limit or shut down debate if it emerges later in the process. Continual revisions and tweaks create confusion for everyone on the team and result in extensive revisions to the proposal document later in the process. If the RFP changes, adjustments are sometimes unavoidable. But every revision cycle consumes time and offers another opportunity to introduce errors.

Step 7: Document and Disseminate

The proposal manager can play a critical role in this step. Solution meetings should result in a document that those who attended the meeting, as well as those who did not, can easily understand. Without documentation, people rely on memory, which is at best imperfect and, in any event, will vary among individuals. This sounds obvious and intuitive, yet many solution meetings conclude without anyone taking responsibility for documenting the decisions and conclusions agreed to. To preclude this possibility, assign someone to be the record-keeper at the beginning of the meeting. Include the rationale for each assumption or decision, and the contending points of view. Otherwise, you are likely to end up revisiting the same debates later.

A solution document might be a revised version of the checklists illustrated above. It could include any previously created artifacts (brochures, specification sheets, proposal sections). It could include maps, charts, diagrams, presentations or spreadsheets.

Store the solution documents in a place that everyone on the team can access and designate one person to update them if some of the components change during the proposal process. Although the solution should stay locked down, some events are out of your control. A product could be discontinued, a subcontractor could go out of business, an amendment to the RFP might change the specifications or a key employee could leave the company.

Then, make sure that the team knows the documentation exists and where to find it. Everyone involved in the proposal should understand, at least at a basic level, what you are offering in the proposal. Administrative, legal, financial and lower-level staff might not participate in solution development, but they should be informed of the results and able to easily access solution documentation.

Conclusion

Proposal managers who engage in solution development and documentation will be very effective in managing the process from RFP release to proposal delivery. It takes extra effort, and the effort pays off.

Note

1 See Vijay Kumar, *101 Design Methods: A Structured Approach for Driving Innovation in Your Organization*, Wiley, October 2012; Dan Roam, *The Back of the Napkin: Solving Problems and Selling Ideas with Pictures*, Portfolio, December 2009; Dave Gray, Sunni Brown, and James Macanufo, *Gamestorming: A Playbook for Innovators, Rulebreakers, and Changemakers*, O'Reilly Media, August 2010.

Chapter 3

Creating the Proposal Outline

Definition

An outline is a hierarchical list of headings (not to be confused with headers, the term used to refer to text that appears in the top margin of the page) to describe the paragraphs that follow them. It is a set of labels. In a simple document, all the headings are at the same level; there are no subheadings or sub-subheadings. In other documents, you might see many layers of headings.

A good proposal outline is similar to the skeletal structure of a person. When bones and joints are weak or misaligned, health and mobility can be difficult or painful, or both. All the activities in this book are foundational. Some of them you can compensate for if you cannot complete them in their entirety. The outline is one activity for which there are no work-arounds, and it is critical to execute all the steps if you want to submit a winning proposal.

> **For the Solo Practitioner**
>
> If you are the only one creating content, a good outline will make this proposal possible for you. As difficult as it might seem, isolate time to develop a compliant outline. If at all possible, find colleagues who can help validate that the way you are developing headings and allocating pages to different topics makes sense.

Why Is it Important?

A document without structure and logic is painful to read and often impossible to understand. Preparing an outline for proposal content prior to writing saves time and can cut down on the number of times that content has to be rewritten or reorganized. It makes the proposal easier for evaluators to score.

DOI: 10.4324/9781003581475-4

An outline is also a snapshot of the major pieces of information in the proposal, which is helpful for ensuring compliance with the instructions on the RFP.

Outlines and headings are critical for two reasons. First, they make life easier for anyone who has to read the proposal (proposal evaluators and internal reviewers) and, second, they make life easier for the writers.

If there were no headings, readers would be confronted with sequential paragraphs of text, "a wall of words," with no way of knowing what is contained in each paragraph or page. It is fine for a novel, but proposals have a specific purpose, and people are not reading them for pleasure. Headings, therefore, function as labels that announce what is in the text. Seeing page after page of text is exciting only to the very few who truly love to read anything and everything. Almost everyone else would prefer to see a label that describes short chunks of text, and most people would prefer as little text as possible – one of the reasons for the limits imposed on the length of proposals.

Proposal evaluators have to assign a quality rating to proposals according to a specific list of topics, so it makes sense to point them to where they can find the relevant material that pertains to that topic.

But the outline is about more than labeling text; it is also about showing the relative importance of different sections. Headings at only one level work fine for short and simple documents. In more complex documents, however, such as proposals, a structured set of headings with multiple levels tells the reader which ideas are primary and which are subordinate. Everyone has a different mental filing system. The way we organize headings conveys how we are addressing and understanding the content.

It helps to look at a simple example. If you had a large collection of periodicals from all over the world and on different topics, you could organize it many different ways. You could organize a catalog according to the publication's origin (US or foreign), date of the latest issue or format (digital or hard copy). Which of these would be major headings, versus subheadings, would depend on how you are going to use the catalog and what is most important. The first example would be most useful to people who only speak certain languages or have specific regional interests, the second would be most useful to people who want to see only the latest magazines, and the third would be most useful to someone who can only access periodicals online.

1. By Place of Origin

    a) US
    b) Europe
    c) Asia
    d) Africa

2. By Date of Publication
    a. Published within the Past Week
    b. Published More Than a Week Ago
    c. Published More Than Two Weeks Ago
    d. Published More Than a Month Ago

3. Format
    a. Digital Only
    b. Hard Copy Only
    c. Digital and Hard Copy

The next level of headings conveys the second most important characteristic of each list. In the list of US periodicals, is format (example 4) or date (example 5) more important? It depends on the purpose of the catalog, of course.

4. By Place of Origin
    a. US
        i. Digital Only
        ii. Hard Copy Only
        iii. Digital and Hard Copy
    b. Europe
    c. Asia
    d. Africa

5. By Place of Origin
    a. US
        i. Published within the Past Week
        ii. Published More Than a Week Ago
        iii. Published More Than Two Weeks Ago
        iv. Published More Than a Month Ago
    b. Europe
    c. Asia
    d. Africa

Each choice communicates a conscious decision about which headings – and, therefore, which topics in a proposal – are more important than others, without the audience having to absorb the content in each paragraph.

If a proposal consists of nothing more than short answers to questions on a form, in that instance, it does not make sense to prepare a separate outline.

But, if the proposal content is more than one- or two-sentence answers to questions embedded in a form, an outline is essential to keep the writing focused and convey the important points within the page limitations.

Challenges

Like the other fundamental activities, creating a proposal outline takes time. It is also a cognitively challenging task because RFPs often contain imprecise or contradictory language. The more people in the buying organization who contribute to an RFP, the more likely it is to speak with multiple voices. Proposal books and courses tend to use simple, well-structured examples when explaining how to do outlines. However, fewer and fewer RFPs can be described as either simple or well structured. For this reason, members of the proposal team can disagree on how a proposal should be organized, what the headings should be, which headings should be major headings and which ones should be subordinate. Often, there is no one perfect answer. When time is short, it can seem as though the outline is a roadblock to forward progress. In fact, it saves time in the long run and avoids unnecessary reworking and reorganization of the proposal.

A related challenge is the assignment of pages to each outline section. Since most proposals are page-limited, the page budget has to be split between different topics. This can be especially difficult if the RFP calls on bidders to address many requirements in a small number of proposal pages.

When Does it Happen?

The creation of the outline occurs the moment there is a draft or final RFP that includes instructions and evaluation criteria. Although it is possible to anticipate what will be in an RFP, without reliable information, the proposal manager risks spending time and energy developing artifacts that will not be required. This can undermine the authority and credibility of the proposal manager. The best practice is to collaborate with the capture manager or anyone else who has knowledge of the customer's environment and timeline.

Who Owns It?

The proposal manager owns the outline and maintains configuration control over it. However, developing the outline is a collaborative effort (see step two below). Multiple team members must buy in and agree to the outline for it to be an effective tool. Otherwise, writers will feel free to ignore it.

Steps in the Process

The steps here apply to proposal sections that require you to create narrative text. If the RFP includes forms, templates with blank spaces that have to be filled in, spreadsheets or any other formatted documents, you do not need an outline for those sections. You should not add headings to RFP forms or templates and you should preserve the format in the RFP as much as possible.

Before describing the steps, it is important to recognize the difference between "compliance-driven" headings and writer-driven headings. Compliance-driven headings correspond directly to specific requirements or instructions in the RFP. As detailed in the chapter on creating proposal content (Chapter 6), writer-driven headings, usually subordinate to the compliance-driven headings, are those that are left to the bidder's discretion. These apply when the proposal contains general instructions, such as "Describe your management approach," without any further detail.

Although it takes time to create a substantive outline with multiple layers, writers find that, once an outline exists, the process of writing sentences and paragraphs goes much faster. Another advantage of using many layers of labels and sentence fragments is that it is easy to spot inconsistencies or incorrect terminology.

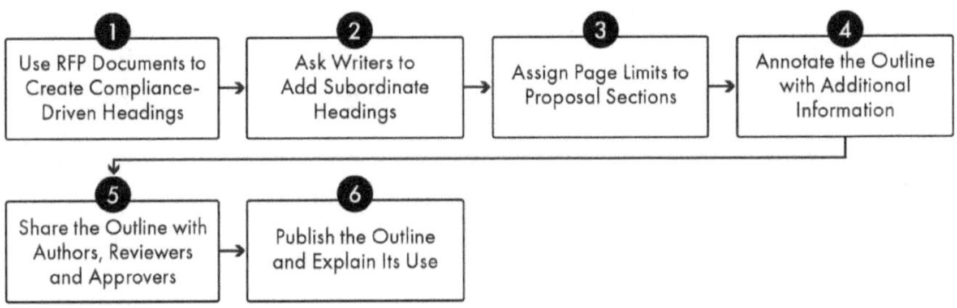

Figure 3.1 Outline

Finally, it is much easier to move headings and fragments than it is to rewrite paragraphs.

Many tools exist to format headings and to move them electronically, but it often helps to use a manual approach such as sticky notes to see the flow of the document across many pages at once.

Creating the outline is a six-step process that can be broken into smaller tasks for large, complicated proposals and compressed in time to accommodate tight deadlines.

Step 1: Use RFP Documents to Create Compliance-Driven Headings

Always begin by following any layout, content or organizational instruction in the RFP. Some RFPs have specific information about headings, subheadings, tabs, appendices and other parts of the document. In these instances, the RFP itself contains the outline. The RFP is always right, even if it does not appear to make sense, because the proposal will be evaluated based on adherence to those instructions.

If the RFP does not instruct bidders where to put the required content within the proposal, make a list of everything that the RFP asks bidders to provide. If the RFP includes a hierarchy of topics, with some subordinate to others, use that exact same hierarchy of headings in your proposal. These constitute the compliance-driven headings of the proposal.

We will start with a simple example and then move on to the more difficult cases. Here are instructions from a typical US government RFP.

PROPOSAL INSTRUCTIONS

Provide a discussion and demonstration of:

1. An understanding of the background, objectives, and work requirements of the PWS/SOW.
2. The proposed methods and techniques for completing the requirements of the solicitation.
3. Provide the information on key personnel (listed in Paragraph 3 of the PWS), such as the principal investigator, unexploded ordinance technician and medical technician.
4. The proposed Management Plan.
5. The proposed Staffing Plan.
6. The proposed Quality Assurance Plan.
7. A description of all proposed teaming partners, use of volunteers and major subcontractors.

The headings for the proposal outline are relatively easy to create because the RFP is prescriptive. The high-level outline would thus likely resemble the following:

1. Background, Objectives and Work Requirements of the Performance Work Statement (PWS)/Statement of Work (SOW);
2. Methods and Techniques for Fulfilling the Requirements;
3. Key Personnel;
4. Management Plan;
5. Staffing Plan Showing Names of Personnel and Hours by Task;
6. Quality Assurance Plan;
7. Teaming Partners, Volunteers and Major Subcontractors.

It often makes sense to truncate the language from the RFP when creating headings, as in the example above, rather than repeating every single word.

Otherwise, headings can take up a lot of space. Sometimes, the instructions for headings are expressed as an entire sentence, such as:

Bidders should clearly explain all aspects of the methods and techniques they propose to use to fulfill the requirements.

In this example, it makes no sense to turn the entire sentence into a heading. By definition, headings should be short and telegraphic or they defeat the purpose and start to resemble the text. This is a strain on the reader. Moreover, headings that take up multiple lines will cut into page count that could be used for more substantive information. So, it would make perfect sense to shorten this sentence into a heading such as:

Methods and Techniques for Fulfilling the Requirements

Whether or not you are condensing a sentence, do not, however, change the wording by inserting your own terminology that you believe to be equivalent. If the RFP asks for "sequential steps in the process," do not use the term "methodology" instead. If they call it a banana, you should call it a banana, even if it is a cupcake. Even if it makes no sense. Even if it is incorrect! The audience for the proposal is the customer, so it is essential to use the customer's language and not the language you think is right. You can educate the customer after you win the award. Using the language from the RFP also makes it easier for someone to check and make sure that all the required elements are in the proposal. In addition to repeating the customer's language, it is important that your headings appear in the same order that they appear in the RFP. Often this is inconvenient, such as when the instructions ask you to place a description of the roles and responsibilities of your key personnel before the project organization chart. Nevertheless, you should stay with the order of the headings in the RFP.

Step 2: Ask Writers to Add Subordinate Headings

In the example above, if the proposal instructions included a ten-page limit, no additional headings would be needed, and the outline would probably be complete.

But, if the proposal in this example had a 50-page limit, it would be smart to create subordinate headings. It is easy for a proposal evaluator to get lost if there are too many pages of text with no headings; very often, the reader forgets what came before and what comes next. A good rule of thumb is that, after each heading, there should be less than one page of text before the next heading or a subordinate heading. This is only a guide. If there are charts, tables, graphics or illustrations, headings might be separated by three or four or more pages. Subordinate headings that are not required by the RFP can always be deleted later, but they force writers to organize and write to a logical structure.

In this example, subordinate headings (added in italics) might look like this:

1. Background, Objectives and Work Requirements of the PWS/SOW
   a. Background
   b. Objectives
   c. Work Requirements
2. Methods and Techniques for Completing the Requirements
   a. Methods
      i. *Previously used methods*
      ii. *Proposed new methods*
      iii. *Results anticipated using new methods*
   b. Techniques
      i. *Previously used techniques*
      ii. *Proposed new techniques*
      iii. *Results anticipated using new techniques*
3. Key Personnel
   a. Program Manager
   b. Deputy Program Manager
   c. Scientist
   d. Engineer
4. Management Plan
   a. Kick-Off Meeting
   b. Schedule
   c. Deliverables
5. Staffing Plan
   a. Personnel and Hours for Task 1
   b. Personnel and Hours for Task 2
   c. Personnel and Hours for Task 3

6. Quality Assurance Plan

    a. *Quality Assurance Roles and Responsibilities*
    b. *Quality Standards*
    c. *Quality Measurement*
    d. *Quality Reporting*
    e. *Continuous Improvement*

7. Teaming Partners, Volunteers and Major Subcontractors

    a. Teaming Partners
    b. Volunteers
    c. Major Subcontractors

In this example, 2.a.i–2.a.iii, as well as other headings in italics, are writer-driven headings. The RFP instructions call for methods and techniques (2.a and 2.b), which are compliance-driven headings, but they do not tell you how to organize the content within your methods or techniques.

In creating subordinate headings, remember the realities of page formatting: each heading takes up space on the page. Some RFPs have so many required topics that there is no room for all the text associated with them. In that scenario, it can be helpful to refer to the topics by the numbered paragraph from the RFP.

Aligning Similar, Parallel Subheadings

Typically, a proposal manager prepares the compliance-driven headings and leaves the writer-driven headings to the writer to complete. There is an exception to this rule, however. If the proposal manager assigns different writers to similar sections, it is essential to ensure coordination so that each one has the same outline. So, in this example, one person might have the assignment to write:

2. Methods and Techniques for Completing the Requirements

    a. Methods

Another writer might have the assignment to write content for:

    b. Techniques

The writer for "a" might want to organize the material one way, and the writer for "b" might choose to organize it differently. So, the resulting outline might look like:

a. Methods

    i. Previously used methods

   ii. Proposed new methods
   iii. Results anticipated using new methods

b. Techniques

   i. Qualitative techniques
   ii. Quantitative techniques
   iii. Technology-driven techniques

This outline is not wrong and it is not non-compliant, because the RFP does not specify how to break down the topic. But it is jarring and potentially confusing to the reader who is trying to follow a logical train of thought. The proposal manager has the responsibility to reach agreement on the best way to structure the content of parallel sections that derive from the same requirement, such as methods and techniques in the example above.

Breaking Up Long Narrative Proposal Instructions

Another instance where the proposal manager, as opposed to the writer, might be the best person to create subordinate headings is when a single instruction contains many topics, as in the sentence:

Explain your subcontractor management approach, including processing of time charges, subcontractor invoices, oversight of subcontractor personnel, changes to subcontractor scope, controlling the quality of subcontractor deliverables and communication among subcontractors.

This is too much information for one heading, and it makes sense to turn all the items starting with the word "subcontractor" into individual subheadings:

b. Subcontractor Management Approach

   i. Processing Time Charges
   ii. Invoices
   iii. Oversight of Subcontractor Personnel
   iv. Changes to Subcontractor Scope
   v. Controlling Quality of Subcontractor Deliverables
   vi. Communication Among Subcontractors

Inconsistencies across RFP Documents or Sections

Large RFPs that were prepared by multiple teams in the customer's organization can be challenging because, often, the teams work independently, and no one checks the RFP documents for consistency. This results in conflicting RFP sections or statements. With a professionally prepared RFP, it should be possible to create an outline in which the major headings are from the instructions (Section L in many federal RFPs), the next-level headings from the evaluation criteria (Section M in many federal RFPs) and the third-level headings from the statement of work. This is the textbook explanation of how to create an outline and it is a logical approach. For example:

4. Management Plan (L.3.4.2)
    4.1 Ability to Keep Project on Budget and Schedule (M.5.3.6)
        a. Kick-Off Meeting (SOW 9.1)
        b. Schedule (SOW 9.2)
        c. Deliverables (SOW 9.3)

But, often, the language and structure of the RFP preclude this option. Here is an example of instructions and evaluation criteria that do not align.

Proposal Instructions

Provide a discussion and demonstration of:

1. An understanding of the background, objectives and work requirements of the SOW.
2. The proposed methods and techniques for completing the requirements of the solicitation.
3. The Information on key personnel (listed in Paragraph 3 of the PWS), such as the principal investigator, unexploded ordinance technician and medical technician.
4. The proposed Management Plan.
5. The proposed Staffing Plan.
6. The proposed Quality Assurance Plan.
7. A description of all proposed teaming partners, use of volunteers and major subcontractors.

Evaluation Criteria

Bidders' proposals will be evaluated on the degree to which they address, in descending order of importance:

- Recruiting, retention and assignment of personnel to tasks.
- Previous relevant contracts.

- Soundness of the technical approach.
- Security measures.

This is clearly an example of multiple people contributing to an RFP without coordinating with each other. Is the instruction to provide methods and techniques the same thing as a technical approach? Maybe. Is assignment of personnel to tasks the same thing as staffing? Yet weaving them into the existing structure creates additional risk.

1. Background, Objectives and Work Requirements of the PWS/SOW
2. Technical Approach
    a. Methods for Fulfilling the Requirements
    b. Techniques for Fulfilling the Requirements
3. Key Personnel
4. Management Plan
    a. Kick-Off Meeting
    b. Schedule
    c. Deliverables
5. Staffing Plan
    a. Recruiting
    b. Retention
    c. Assignment of Personnel to Tasks 1, 2 and 3
6. Quality Assurance Plan
7. Teaming Partners, Volunteers, and Major Subcontractors
8. Previous Relevant Contracts
9. Security Measures

This structure creates confusion because the evaluation factors (in bold) are now not in the order in which they appear in the RFP, and they are at different levels of the outline, making them difficult to find. If we add each of the evaluation factors in bold to the end of the outline as separate headings, we are going to be repeating material already covered. Often, page limits preclude this option.

More Requirements than the Page Limit Allows

An overwhelming number of requirements is a different challenge. It is common to find statements in an RFP directing the bidders to write about their approach to 50, 75 or more pages of requirements in 20 or 25 pages of proposal copy, as in this example:

Instructions for Section 1
Explain your technical approach, addressing each of the SOW requirements in detail.
Page limit: 20
[The attached SOW has over 200 separate requirements.]

Several techniques are available to address this challenge. The first is to bundle requirements and address them all together. This assumes that the engineers, subject matter experts or business development staff understand the work well enough to know which items can be grouped together. Are there 25, 30 or more requirements that can all be met using the same tool or approach? If the RFP paragraphs are numbered, it makes it easier to refer to all of them in a table (see Table 3.1).

It is not a simple matter to execute this approach if the team is not intimately familiar with the SOW. The second, complementary, approach is to identify the requirements that are the most critical from the customer's perspective and devote most of the space to those, while summarizing the others.

This example demonstrates why creating a proposal outline is a difficult conceptual task and not a strictly mechanical one. There is no perfect solution here. One option that leaves the structure prescribed by the instructions intact is to create a table that lists the evaluation factors and the proposal section(s) where each one is addressed. The example also shows the importance of preparing the outline as early in the proposal process as possible. In this instance, it might have been possible to ask a question about the RFP that would have resulted in a revised RFP that resolved the disconnect between the instructions and the evaluation factors.

Table 3.1 Technical Approach Summary

Requirements	*Approach*
SOW 3.1–3.7, 5.7, 8.1	Display real-time data on dashboard that contains links for feedback and corrective actions
SOW 3.8, 5.1–5.6, 8.2–8.8	Conduct daily status meetings to review critical metrics
SOW 1, 2, 3.9, 5.8, 8.9	Engage SMEs to review content prior to preparing deliverables

Step 3: Assign Page Limits

Many RFPs prescribe an exact number of pages for each major heading. The page limits dictated by the RFP should be documented in the outline. If the RFP does not limit the number of pages, or if the limits apply to the sum of the pages in multiple sections, such as a 50-page limit for a volume with many sections in it, it is a good idea to self-impose limits on each section and subsection. Typically, the degree of importance of an RFP requirement is the best starting place for assigning page limits. Many RFPs indicate which requirements are more important than others. For example, if the quality control plan is only half as important in the evaluation process as the staffing plan, it would make sense to allocate fewer pages to it. However, there are always exceptions here too. The staffing plan might require more pages because of the number of positions.

If a proposal or a proposal section has no page limit specified in the RFP, and there are no evaluation criteria to use as a guide, you can assign a limit based on the amount of time available for writing proposal content. Descriptive prose and graphics (these do not include resumes, certification forms, pricing tables or other standard content that probably already exists in some form) take time to create. Really good writers can generate four pages a day of new copy for a first draft. If the content is similar to prose that has been used in previous proposals, the output increases to approximately twice that amount. In practice, it is rare that entire paragraphs or even sentences can be, or should be, used in their entirety, without revision. Thus, a 50-page proposal will probably take five people at least three to four days to write. This does not include time for integration of the different sections, review of the content or incorporation of suggestions for improvement, which typically take as much time as the creation of the first draft.

Although it is possible to produce more pages by adding more writers, adding writers often adds time to the schedule because of the challenge entailed in integrating different styles and making content consistent across proposal sections. So, although it seems as though it would save time, asking ten people to each write five pages is not faster than asking five people to each write ten pages.

Step 4: Annotate the Outline with Additional Information

Most RFPs have both page numbers and numbered headings. Each compliance-driven heading in the outline should be followed by a reference to where the heading is addressed in the RFP. There can be multiple references for any given heading. Typically, the annotations look something like this:

1. Background, Objectives and Work Requirements of the PWS/SOW (L.4.1)
   a. Background (L.4.1.1)
   b. Objectives (L.4.1.2)
   c. Work Requirements (L.4.1.3, PWS 3.1–3.12)

Some proposal managers add the section due date, the writer's name and other information to the outline. This makes sense as long as the information is not already documented somewhere else, in which case, when things change, the information has to be updated in two places.

Step 5: Share the Outline with Writers, Reviewers and Approvers

On complicated US federal government bids, the process of reaching agreement on the best outline to use can take days, if not longer. On short, simple proposals, it might take less than an hour. Either way, it is essential to get buy-in before writers start creating content. If a senior executive reads the proposal late in the process and decides the proposal should be reorganized, the amount of extra effort to do this can be daunting, and it might come at the expense of important compliance checks and improvements in the content. Continue to share with everyone involved until you get formal agreement from anyone who has the authority to direct a reorganization later on. Do not assume that reviewers and approvers have no objections simply because they remain silent.

Make sure everyone understands that, once the outline is approved, it does not change unless there is a revision to the RFP, in which case the proposal manager should go through the approval process again. Once writers start creating text and graphics with an organizing principle in mind, it is both difficult and time-consuming to change course. It is better to spend the extra time at the beginning of the proposal making sure that the outline makes sense to all the writers than to start down one path and then change direction.

Amendments, revisions to the RFP and answers to questions can all force changes to the outline. Writers sometimes find that the structure is awkward or does not flow and they ask that the outline be changed. The problem is that every change creates the potential for confusion, reworking and errors. So, it is important to only change the outline when absolutely necessary and when all the important contributors (writers, reviewers, people in the proposal chain) agree on the changes.

"As the senior person here, I recommend you throw out this draft and completely reorganize it. It won't take too long if you follow my advice and put your mind to it."

Step 6: Publish the Outline and Explain Its Use

Once you have reached agreement on the outline, publish it to a collaborative site or whatever document library you use for important artifacts such as the RFP, the schedule and the contact list. Confirm that each writer understands the headings and that everyone knows the outline should not change without coordination by the proposal manager. Otherwise, some writers might see the outline as a suggestion and not a command.

Conclusion

The outline is foundational because changing the organization of the proposal is extremely costly in time and morale. Outlines require collaboration; they can be open to interpretation; they are time-consuming; and they can be cognitively difficult. Sometimes, the result is a compromise between less-than-perfect alternatives. The important principle is to maintain traceability back to the RFP, so that the headings and subheadings are all defensible as compliant and based on the same logic.

Chapter 4

Assembling a Proposal Team and Making Assignments

Definition

This activity entails breaking the proposal process into discrete tasks, defining the tasks clearly and setting performance objectives, deciding who is going to do what and getting people to commit to each task. A short, simple proposal might have a team of one, yet defining the tasks and getting a commitment for small proposals is just as important as for large, complicated ones with experts from different fields and departments, numbering 10, 20 or more people.

Why Is it Important?

The first reason that this step is fundamental is the unforgiving proposal schedule. Having the right team in place ultimately saves precious time. Because tasks are highly interdependent and deadline-driven, there is no time to recover if one task falls short of what is needed. For example, if a subcontracts manager does not clearly explain what is required of a subcontractor's bid, and the subcontractor submits a bid for the wrong services at the wrong price, there might not be time to get the correct bid. Interdependence between tasks means that the wrong subcontractor bid is likely to affect the proposal solution and price, which in turn can cause a delay in proposal reviews and final production. A last-minute rush to finish often results in failing to see errors or introducing new ones.

Being deliberate and specific about this step is essential for another reason. Proposals invariably include people who have different proposal experiences. A proposal writer, for example, might assume that someone will provide a template that includes all the proposal headings in the correct format. At the same time, the proposal manager might prefer to receive unformatted text that a professional desktop publisher can put into a template.

The clock keeps ticking, meanwhile, the writer is waiting for a template to get started, and the proposal manager is waiting to get text to put into a template. This is just one of many misunderstandings that

DOI: 10.4324/9781003581475-5

can occur without clear role and process definition. Without clear direction, people will revert to what they assume or what they know how to do. Some team members will do less than the proposal manager expects; others might do more and inadvertently replicate work that someone else is doing. Even if the team is composed of people who have worked together before in similar roles, each RFP and each opportunity is different. A small detail, such as a restriction on the size of the font or the margins, can dramatically affect how individuals complete their tasks, and there are always people who are participating in a proposal for the first time. They cannot possibly be successful without clear direction and instructions.

Challenges

The first challenge in assembling a team is that the proposal manager rarely has authority over any of the potential participants. Without authority, it is difficult to make demands and hold people accountable. Buy-in and backing from senior managers is essential.

A second difficulty is a tendency to conflate three distinct activities: defining roles, assigning someone to each role and explaining what each role entails. Each takes time, and each is difficult for a different reason. As proposal managers, it is our job to define roles. But, because we live and breathe and eat and sleep proposals, it is easy to skip over role definitions in the interest of moving the schedule along. Because we know what a volume lead is, we assume everyone does. Making assignments is not the job of the proposal manager. A proposal manager can sometimes make recommendations as to who might play a given role but typically cannot make formal role assignments. This is the job of someone senior enough in the organization to command authority. It might be the capture manager or it might be another executive.

When you are not clear about who is making the assignment, you can end up with the following scenario.

Proposal Manager:	Who can take ownership of the key personnel resumes?
Capture Manager:	I know that Sally can do it. She owes me! And resumes are not that hard anyway. It's not that big a deal. [They are hard, and it is a big deal, but that is a subject for another book!]
Proposal Manager:	Have you talked to her?
Capture Manager:	No. I don't need to talk to her. She has done this before. Just send her an email and tell her to read the RFP. She will come through for us.

Proposal Manager: When is the last time you worked with her?
Capture Manager: Don't worry. She has been around forever and she knows this proposal stuff backwards and forwards.

You can see where this conversation is going, and what is likely to result.

An aggravating factor is that Sally, assuming she really is the best person for the job, is very likely to have a "day" job (possibly multiple day jobs) and other commitments. The capture manager probably has little insight into her workload. Sally might not be the best person after all. Even when the capture manager agrees to make assignments personally, because the most qualified people are often also the most over-committed, capture managers are sometimes only able to get agreement by pleading and cajoling. The participant then feels that this is a favor and not a commitment.

Explaining the details of a role, likewise, is not easy. Proposal managers are often hesitant to walk through all the specifics of a role with someone more senior, possibly someone who has been involved in many other previous proposals. These can be awkward conversations. People do not like to talk about details. It is boring to talk about how to name files, what is in the different RFP sections, what meetings to attend, what deadlines have to be met. Proposal managers have a justified fear of appearing to be condescending.

When Does it Happen?

In an ideal world, proposal managers clarify and confirm assignments after the team has carefully analyzed the RFP, submitted questions and clearly articulated and documented a solution. Most proposal response times do not permit that. This activity can occur any time after the proposal manager has completed a shred and understands exactly what content is required to deliver a compliant proposal. For some proposals, that could be within hours of receiving the RFP. It should always occur before people start creating proposal content. With good advance knowledge of what will be in the RFP, it is possible, and sometimes advisable, to make tentative plans and assignments in advance, with the understanding that everything can change when there is a final solicitation.

Who Owns it?

The proposal manager has to make sure that this activity takes place but cannot entirely control it. Almost every proposal manager will need or want support from executives in carrying it out. In many organizations, certain roles are defined well before the proposal manager gets involved.

Steps in the Process

When it comes to team assignments, proposal managers inherit a range of different situations. Sometimes, we engage with a team that is already formed, or partially formed, with some roles assigned. Other times, we are asked to build a team. The best scenario is when we can work in concert with the capture manager or another senior executive to identify the right people and clarify roles. The six steps here assume that you are in this best scenario. If you are not, and if you have inherited a team, or part of a team, adjust these steps to accommodate your situation and accept the reality that there might be roles or assignments you cannot control. You might want to first assess the role definitions and assignments that are already in place before presenting your own estimate to a capture manager (step four). The meeting with the capture manager can be used to validate the assignments and gain information about why the individuals were chosen and what the assumptions are. Regardless, it is worth thinking through the detailed steps to complete each proposal activity.

The way to address the multiple challenges associated with forming a team and defining responsibilities is to be deliberate and specific, even at the risk of over-communicating. The steps here apply for both large and small teams. In fact, it is probably even more important to go through the steps with small teams composed of members who already know each other. In that scenario, it is easy to make assumptions and skip over important details.

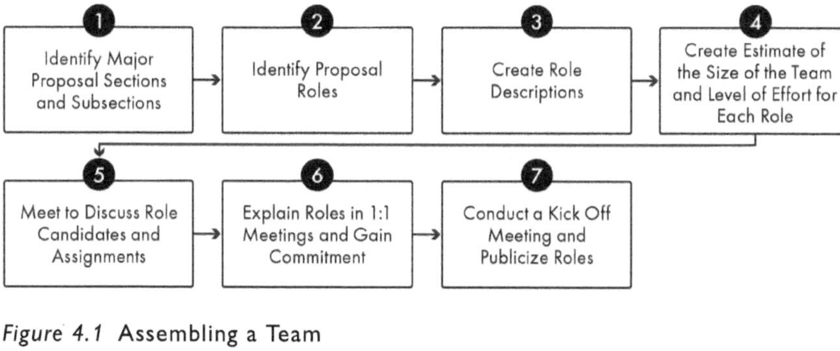

Figure 4.1 Assembling a Team

Step 1: Identify Major Proposal Sections and Subsections

Using either the shred or the RFP itself, identify each of the required proposal sections. If you have not yet had time to create a proposal outline, this step will help with that activity as well. For most proposals, the list of sections looks something like this:

- Executive Summary;
- Technical Approach;
- Management Plan;
- Staffing Plan;
- Resumes;
- Quality Control Plan;
- Pricing Tables;
- Price Narrative;
- Assumptions;
- Contractual Representations.

Be sure to capture every single item that has to be submitted as part of your proposal, including a cover letter, forms, tables, letters of commitment, master table of contents, legal disclosures and signature pages. Do not limit the list to the technical and management sections. Although instructions are often in one place in the RFP, they can be buried anywhere. I once found a reference to a required quality control plan in an appendix, and it would have been easy to miss because this RFP had more than 20 appendices. In US federal government RFPs, required proposal content sometimes shows up in Section G (Special Contract Requirements) or Section F (Deliveries or Performance). The best way to make sure that you are capturing everything is to do a word search for the word "proposal" in all the RFP documents.

Step 2: Identify Proposal Roles

Once you have a list of all the items that you will have to submit, make a list of the key proposal roles. Many different types of participants contribute to the process. On most proposals, there are:

- Sponsors – the people who have asked for proposal services; often the corporate department whose products or services form the solution or offering;

For the Solo Practitioner

Although it can seem overwhelming, list the separate functions to be performed, even though you might be performing all of them. You might decide that responding is beyond your capability and your time

- Approvers – often senior executives in the organization; there might be different levels and types of approvals for different proposal deliverables;
- Owners – these are people who create or supervise proposal content development and are accountable for delivering it on schedule. Each proposal section should have an owner other than the proposal manager. For smaller, simpler proposals, multiple sections can have the same owner;
- Reviewers – people who read the proposal to make sure it is accurate, compliant and compelling. Reviewers are often sponsors or approvers;
- Production team members – people who format, edit and print proposal sections;
- Legal, security and financial experts – people who populate pricing forms and documents and who review RFP and proposal content for legal implications.

and energy are better spent elsewhere.

- Consider engaging help, even if it means calling in favors or investing in external expertise, especially for proposal reviews, editing and formatting. These are functions which are very difficult to do on your own, with no support.
- Make sure you have the time and energy to do all of them.
- Ask friends and colleagues for assistance where you have questions or where you can benefit from a fresh set of eyes.

Your proposal might require other functions such as logistics, human resources, risk management, procurement, subcontracting or competitor analysis. If you are not sure your list is complete, consult with someone who has experience on similar bids. Do not ignore a role simply because you do not know who can fill it.

Step 3: Create Role Descriptions

For each section or function, create a detailed description of the role or review the role description that exists. If you have a small team – for example, two or three people – it is tempting to skip this step and assume everyone knows what to do. Do not skip it. Each RFP is unique, and people forget what they are supposed to do from one proposal to the next. It is impossible to over-communicate during the proposal process. Errors inevitably result from general, vague or insufficient communication.

Some roles will be easy to describe with few words. For example:

Write a three-page description of how we will keep the project on schedule and within budget. Complete the first draft by Tuesday, August 4. Incorporate changes suggested by reviewers no later than August 12.

Other roles have more steps. Preparing resumes, for example, is a multi-step activity that is often the stepchild of the proposal, assigned to a junior person, because no one has bothered to decompose it. The description of that role will be longer and more detailed:

- Create resume template based on RFP for approval by proposal manager;
- Secure approval or make necessary adjustments to template;
- Collect pre-existing resumes;
- Review for responsiveness to personnel qualifications in RFP or desired strengths;
- Interview personnel to close any gaps;
- Identify personnel who cannot meet the requirements and find replacement;
- Edit/rewrite resumes as necessary;
- Send resumes back to personnel for approval/changes;
- Have resumes put into approved template;
- Complete resumes in time for color reviews;
- Participate in color team debriefs;
- Revise resumes as required by color team comments;
- Get signatures and consent letters;
- Send final version to desktop publisher.

Decomposing the role shows that it might not be best to give this assignment to a junior person, particularly if your proposals entail delivering a service, because services are all about the people. Resumes can count for a lot.

Create a list of expectations that apply to all proposal team members or review whatever corporate policies and procedures apply to proposal team management. Common expectations are regular participation in daily calls, prompt return of phone calls and emails, communication with the proposal manager about issues before they spiral out of control, monitoring and returning emails within a reasonable time frame and rapid escalation of issues before they derail the proposal schedule.

Step 4: Create an Estimate of the Size of the Team and the Level of Effort Required for Each Role

Good role definition will enable you to decide how many people should be on the team. Start with the proposal sections and determine how many section owners you will need. The concept of ownership is key. Owners are accountable for delivering a finished section or volume. They might write all of it. Or they might not write any of it and instead direct, integrate and check the work of multiple writers. When a section calls for multiple different types of content and expertise, it is rare that one person can write it, but it is essential that one person own it.

Each section should have only one owner. Shared ownership does not work when there are tight deadlines and precise requirements. Just because each section has to have one owner, does not mean that one person cannot own several sections. On small proposals, one person might be able to manage both the staffing plan and the resumes. However, if you have to submit dozens of resumes and a staffing plan that covers hundreds of people over multiple years, the job is probably too much for one person. That is why determining the level of effort is key. In estimating how many section owners you need, remember that sections can include cover letters, forms, acronym lists, compliance matrices, consent letters, as well as other items. The owner does not have to personally prepare each of these items but is accountable for seeing that they are prepared and checked for accuracy.

There is no magic formula that dictates how many pages of a proposal one person can own. An experienced professional can delegate work, integrate the contributions of others efficiently and easily assemble sections that are 50, 75 or more pages. Professionals with no proposal experience might struggle owning a five-page section on a relatively simple topic.

Estimating how many people you will need will depend heavily on the amount of time you have to prepare the proposal. A shorter time frame often means engaging more people. However, chopping the work into ever smaller pieces and engaging more and more people do not necessarily make for efficiency and often make the work take longer. If a proposal section is going to be 50 pages, it might make sense to assign five people 10 pages each. But it would not make sense to assign 25 people two pages each. The work of tracking progress and integrating the drafts would outweigh any efficiencies.

Once you know how many section owners you require, determine how much work will be assigned to the people who perform proposal administrative and support functions, such as reviewing the documents for accuracy, editing, formatting, arranging proposal reviews, arranging meetings, maintaining documents and communicating with the team. Do the same for the additional support required from other departments such as human resources, purchasing, subcontracting and security. Each of those functions should also have only one owner, even if the function will require more than one person. For example, if the final proposal document is going to be hundreds of pages long, it is not realistic to expect that one editor or one desktop publisher will be enough. But you should designate a lead editor and a lead desktop publisher. Industry metrics can be very helpful here, since they will help you calculate how many people you will need to execute these functions. For example, updating a graphic with new content typically takes two to four hours per graphic. Desktop publishers can format 20–50 pages an hour, depending on how clean the material is.

As you are developing estimates, state your assumptions about the skills of the person who will occupy the role. Make a note of the level of skills and experience connected to each role. Reviewers might need specific knowledge, clearances, subject matter expertise or exposure to the customer. RFPs sometimes require proposal content that is formatted using specific software packages, or content that is approved by someone with certain certifications. Every proposal is different, but Table 4.1 indicates what an estimate might resemble for a hypothetical proposal.

Table 4.1 Typical Proposal Roles

Role	*Abbreviated Role Description*	*Estimate/Comments*
Resume owner	Prepare resumes in approved template for four key and seven non-key personnel in time for color reviews	One experienced proposal professional
Technical approach section owner	Populate 50-page section that describes features and benefits of solution in time for color reviews	Owner will have to delegate to three or four others who will work half-time or less for two weeks; owner will work half-time for two weeks and full-time for one week
Technical approach section writer	Write content per direction from section owner and proposal manager; due on February 5	Four writers; ten pages assigned to each one
Quality control plan owner	Prepare five-page QC plan in accordance with RFP instructions in time for color reviews	One senior subject matter expert
Pricing expert	Populate pricing spreadsheets; write pricing assumptions; write cost narrative	One experienced proposal pricer
Red team reviewers	Read proposal draft for accuracy, omissions, incorporation of compelling messages, consistency	Four or five senior people who have the time to read the RFP carefully and perform a thorough review within a tight time frame (eight to ten hours)
Editor	Deep copy edit of all resumes, technical approach section and quality control plan	One senior editor with proposal experience who can be available to work full-time as well as evenings and weekends
Desktop publisher	Create document template and format final copy	Two experienced desktop publishers who can work quickly and under pressure

Remember that everyone on the team will be involved in analyzing the RFP and developing questions and make sure the estimate includes time for this activity.

Determining how much work is involved in each proposal section and each function requires experience and judgment. These are not simple calculations. If you do not know the right level of effort for a section or a function, get help from people who have performed the role before. Share the RFP and ask for their opinion on how long it will take to prepare a transition plan, a quality control plan, a staffing plan, a basis of estimate, a security plan or any other item you are not familiar with. Find someone who has managed a proposal that had a similar structure. Asking questions of experts at this point in the process will pay you back many times over. It can be difficult to add staff to a task once the proposal work has started.

Step 5: Meet to Discuss Role Candidates and Assignments

Ask for a face-to-face meeting with the capture manager, department manager or whoever has the authority to assign the right person to each role. This meeting could involve more than one executive, since proposal teams often draw from different departments and levels within a company. In-person meetings are not always possible, and a video call can substitute when necessary. But do not, under any circumstances, attempt to have a discussion about role assignments via email. The possibilities for miscommunication and misunderstanding are endless.

Come to the meeting prepared with your role descriptions for discussion and your best guess as to how much work is going to be required. Ask for confirmation that your estimates are accurate and realistic. Then, discuss candidates for each role. Assess strengths, weaknesses and tradeoffs. If one person is going to own hundreds of pages, who will engage the other supporting players? Does the owner have the leadership and organizational skills to manage a team of contributors? What level of proposal experience does the person have?

Be wary of the candidate whose main qualification is availability. The available person is not necessarily the right person. Ideally, the discussion of assignments is collaborative and non-confrontational, since everyone has a lot to lose if the person chosen is not right for the role. If you do not know the candidates being proposed, ask for their history. Have they worked on proposals before? How recently? Large proposal teams invariably include a few newbies whose managers want them to get training. Although everyone has to start somewhere, high-intensity proposals with tight deadlines are not good training opportunities, and, often, junior people who learn that way also learn that they never want to go near another proposal again.

If you inherit a team, or a partial team, confirm that the candidates already chosen are the right ones for the roles assigned based on your assessment of the level of effort required. The person who made the initial assignment might not share your definition of the proposal roles.

Once you have agreed on the number of people and the best candidates, either confirm that the capture manager has already assigned the role or ask the capture manager to call or meet with each individual (the preferred approach), make the formal assignment and then confirm with you that each person accepted the role.

If you end the meeting with roles unassigned, get a commitment as to how and when the gaps will be filled. Maybe other executives need to be consulted or involved. Maybe the role requires redefinition or clarification. It is not necessary to fill every single role right at the beginning of every proposal. Some functions, such as formatting and editing, are less important early in the process. But it is important to get a commitment as to when proposal staffing will be complete and stick to that date.

At this meeting, be sure to address escalation paths. If the senior engineer or solution architect wants to use one subcontractor, and the business development manager disagrees, who will be the referee, and how will they adjudicate? What will be the process for removing someone from the proposal team? This is not about creating trouble where none exists; it is about a shared understanding of contingencies that are almost certain to occur.

You will want to calibrate your approach to this meeting, depending on the people who attend. If you are meeting with a capture manager you have just finished working with on another proposal, you can reference role descriptions from your experience together, and it is less important to walk through all the specifics. If you do not know the capture manager or other executives, find out how much proposal experience they have and share your role descriptions. Even if they have a lot of proposal experience, their idea of a proposal coordinator or an editor might not be the same as yours. If they do not have a lot of proposal experience, the details of the role are even more important. They cannot identify candidates or make assignments without understanding the work involved.

Defining the roles and meeting with the relevant executives take time, but they will take less time if you do your homework and show up prepared. Moreover, course correction after a bad assignment not only is more time-consuming but is painful in other ways and can needlessly destroy professional relationships.

Step 6: Explain Roles in One-on-One Meetings and Gain Commitments

The final step before the kick-off meeting is to have a conversation with each person on the proposal team who owns a proposal section or function. There are two objectives for this conversation: first, to make sure that both you and the person assigned have the same understanding of what the process is and what constitutes "done." The second is to get a verbal commitment to the role from the person you are meeting with.

For some roles and some people, this can be a very short conversation. If a person's only role is to populate a form, you can probably cover the specifics in a few minutes. The job consists of filling out the form, checking for accuracy and submitting by a certain deadline. But do not forget to get the verbal commitment. A verbal commitment is "yes, I understand what is involved and agree to do the work" or similar words. It is not "ok" or "I'll look into it" or "I'll get back to you."

When the role is more complicated, the way to approach this conversation depends on how senior the person is and the nature of your relationship. A meeting with a senior engineer or subject matter expert with a lot of proposal experience will be different from a conversation with someone who is new to the proposal process. It can be intimidating for a proposal manager to approach a senior engineer with years of proposal experience. Explaining all the steps in the process to someone at that level is perhaps not the best approach. This is why I use questions to frame these conversations. You can use phrases such as:

I know you have done this many times. But I have not. Can you give me a sense of how you go about compiling the quality control plan?

I have seen people create resumes in different ways. What steps do you follow?

Do you normally start with an outline that has at least four or five levels of headings?

Questions like these will tease out the person's process. You can compare what they are saying with the role definition you have created and make a note of any additions or corrections. I always learn something from these conversations, because everyone goes about the assignment in a slightly different way.

Be on the lookout for several warning signs. The first is a refusal to have the meeting at all. This is a clear sign that the person is not taking the assignment seriously and it calls for immediate escalation. The next one is overconfidence. Whenever the person I am talking to tries to cut the meeting short with phrases such as "gotcha" or "no problem; I've got this," I

"We don't need a meeting to discuss this!
Anyone can fill out a workbook with 20 or 30 worksheets."

am pretty sure that the person does not "have" it at all. The third warning sign is when someone describes the process in general terms ("I look at the RFP and then I just write the section") or engages in a theoretical discussion that has little to do with putting words on paper. In my experience, competent and experienced professionals who know how to fill out the form or write the section, regardless of their level of seniority within the organization, are more than happy to explain how they do it in detail. Amateurs tend towards hand-waving and dismissing the conversation as beneath them; experts love specifics and details. As they say in military circles, amateurs discuss strategy; experts discuss logistics.

The response to these warning signs will differ depending on your relationships and on the timeline. If the timeline permits, you can wait and see if the person meets the first deadline. If the function is critical and the timeline is short, you have to escalate by going back to the person who made the assignment in the first place to discuss the concern.

If the person you are meeting with has limited proposal experience and admits to not knowing what the process is, you can use your role description, and you will be glad that you put in the work in the first place.

In an ideal world, these are face-to-face meetings. Body language, gestures and eye contact are all valuable clues about whether the person you are talking to is really signing up for the assignment, or just going through the motions. If you cannot meet in-person, a video teleconference is by far the best option. You will be able to make eye contact, see facial expression, hear tone of voice, and detect whether the person is multi-tasking (another serious warning sign!) while talking to you. A phone call is the least desirable alternative, and email is not an option for this communication. It has to be two-way, and it has to conclude with a "yes, I understand and will do it" or similar phrase.

Step 7: Conduct a Kick-Off Meeting and Publicize Roles

Every proposal should have a kick-off meeting attended by everyone who has a role. The artifacts from this meeting constitute important reference documents for the entire team. If you have followed the previous steps, confirmation of roles at the kick-off meeting will be routine because team members will already know what they have signed up and committed to. All too often, participants are learning about their roles for the first time at the kick-off meeting, and then explanations about what is expected are discussed later, sometimes when it is too late. At the kick-off meeting, the business development or capture executive should explain the background of the opportunity, the purpose of the contract or project, the history with the customer and any known customer likes or sensitivities. It you know who is going to own the solution development activity (see Chapter 2), that person should present a summary of the product, services, system or methodology that is going to be proposed. The rest of the kick-off meeting agenda depends on when you schedule the meeting. It is always best to present the proposal outline and the schedule, with major milestones and recurring meetings, as well as rules of the road for communication and meetings. However, sometimes it is critical for the team to start on certain activities before these artifacts are ready, and, while every proposal should have a kick-off meeting, there are instances when it is not possible owing to tight deadlines, crowded schedules, differing time zones and other logistics. In this scenario, the proposal manager has to make sure that all the contributors receive the same information about the proposal process and the opportunity, and has to bend over backwards to communicate regularly with participants in the most efficient way possible.

Even if you conduct the meeting after having gained clear verbal commitments to well-defined roles, be prepared to adjust assignments mid-course. While this is not something to be encouraged unless necessary, things happen. People have emergencies. The wrong person gets assigned to a role owing to incorrect information. The RFP requirements change. When that happens, be sure that a full explanation of the role is given to the replacement, and that there is a clean hand-off. I managed a proposal several years ago and had to assign my role to a proposal manager colleague mid-course owing to a family emergency. I went to her office and I said "I have been the proposal manager, but I am throwing the ball to you." I even pretended to throw a ball! She said "Yes! I have caught it." *That* is a clean hand-off and a real verbal commitment. That is what enables proposal managers to sleep at night.

Conclusion: Getting Buy-In from the Team Early

The steps outlined here take time and consume energy; each depends on the proposal manager getting information, agreement and commitment from others. It is tempting to skip them for multiple reasons. The steps described here all entail making explicit expectations that people typically assume are shared and understood without being articulated. These unspoken expectations can create significant tension later if not addressed at the outset. Proposal management is still a relatively new profession, and definitions of roles can vary greatly from one organization to another and even within an organization. In some companies, for example, the proposal coordinator performs most of the clerical tasks, such as setting up calendar appointments, posting files and maintaining distribution lists. In others, the coordinator is only involved in granting access to the collaborative IT platform and escalating technical issues; everything else is the proposal manager's responsibility. Some proposal managers function as leaders and as deputy capture managers; others have a much more administrative role. Although formal definitions exist, they leave much room for interpretation.

Moreover, it can feel awkward to state what some people consider obvious, and it is natural to want to avoid appearing condescending, particularly when talking to senior professionals. One approach is to use humor to persuade people that it is worth having very granular conversations about roles. You might say, for example, "I know I am a dunderhead about these things, but I have to understand the details so that I can figure out how to schedule meetings and deadlines." Or: "Back when I went to proposal school, we were taught that you always .... That lesson was pounded into my head and I can't get it out." Self-deprecation lightens the mood, although it is often not necessary. I have found even the most experienced professionals grateful for the opportunity to clarify what they are signing up to, and many are interested in discussing the process in detail so they can perform their roles more effectively.

Chapter 5

The Proposal Schedule

Definition

The proposal schedule is a document that lays out all the milestones between when you receive the RFP and the date and time the proposal is due. Multiple formats and tools exist to create and share the schedule, and no single tool is the best for all situations and teams. I like to keep a very detailed schedule that includes all the interim steps, such as setting up a collaborative site, burning and checking CDs, confirming the delivery and receipt of past performance questionnaires and sending out data requests to subcontractors. However, I do not always share all those details with the entire team.

I did not try to include in this chapter all the specific activities that you will have to schedule, because they differ for each proposal. I address how to sequence the seven fundamental activities covered in this book, principles for scheduling other activities and tips on enforcing the schedule, since all the work to create a plan is wasted if you cannot execute it.

Why Is it Important?

Proposal deadlines are unforgiving because, in a competitive bidding system, the same rules have to apply to all the bidders. If a proposal is due at 10:00 am and a company delivers it at 10:01 am, the customer cannot accept it. Accepting it would mean giving that one company one minute longer to work on the proposal than the other companies, and that would be seen as unfair.

The result of this is that late delivery is the one mistake that guarantees that the bid will be unsuccessful. This is why scheduling is so critical. If the schedule is flawed, or if the team does not adhere to it, all the rest of the effort and investment to win the contract or the sale, which can involve a lead time of months or years, will be sacrificed. This is the single point of failure.

DOI: 10.4324/9781003581475-6

Challenges

Many organizations expect proposal managers to create a schedule almost as soon as they receive the RFP. Creating a realistic schedule that you can enforce takes time, and publishing a bad schedule that you have to constantly revise is counterproductive. That is the first challenge.

The second one is the need for redundancy. Because the risk of a late delivery is not acceptable, the proposal schedule has redundancy built into it. The proposal manager has to check the content on a regular basis, because finding out about an error or omission late in the process often means not having enough time to fix it. Of course, when you stop to check, you lose time. But, if you do not perform those checks, and you find something missing at the end, there is no time to fix it and still meet the deadline. So, the very thing that you need to do to make sure you are on time is, itself, actually time-consuming.

The third is the high degree of collaboration inherent in most proposals. Often, they entail contributions from subject matter experts, editors, graphic artists, legal experts, financial analysts and senior executives. The more different perspectives and contributors, the better the proposal document in the end, and the more different perspectives and people involved, the more time it takes to incorporate all those perspectives, have all those individuals read and comment on the document, and coordinate, communicate and reach consensus. So, the very thing that makes the proposal better also takes more time.

The next challenge is finding the right balance between over-planning and under-planning. It is easy to both over-plan and under-plan when creating a proposal schedule. Under-planning occurs when you do not anticipate contingencies. The rest of life does not stop while the team is creating the proposal. People get sick, have household emergencies, attend to their families, get caught in traffic or sit on planes that never leave the runway. Weather and traffic conditions cause delays. Communications can be interrupted. Equipment can fail. If you do not plan for any of these events, the risk of not delivering on time is high, because one or more are guaranteed to occur. At the same time, it is rare that all these contingencies occur on any one proposal. An over-planned schedule is one that tries to accommodate all of these contingencies, and it is one that leaves no time to actually create and deliver the proposal.

When Does it Happen?

The creation of the schedule is, ideally, the first event. However, sometimes you will have to submit questions on the RFP before you have time to create a schedule. Build the schedule and share it as soon as you can, but not without going through the steps outlined here. If you rush it, you will make mistakes and have to adjust the schedule. This creates havoc for the team, particularly if it is a large team, and undermines your authority as proposal manager.

Who Owns it?

The proposal manager owns the schedule. That does not mean that the proposal manager makes unilateral decisions. Many people provide input, which is why it is not a good idea to rush this activity.

Steps in the Process

Preparing a realistic schedule requires conceptual and practical knowledge. Developing the schedule is highly interdependent with assembling the proposal team and defining roles, since the number of people involved will affect how much time it takes to accomplish certain tasks.

Creating the schedule means remaining aware of the distinction between duration and elapsed time, and Brooks's Law, which addresses the relationship between the number of people working on a task and the time it takes to complete it.

Duration refers to the amount of time an individual spends on a task, and elapsed time is the amount of time before an action is complete. It might take less than two minutes of a person's time to load a dishwasher and an hour before the dishes are actually clean. Additional effort on the part of the person will not make the dishwasher work any faster. The elapsed time is still an hour, even though the personal effort involved is less than two minutes. On a proposal, some tasks require a certain amount

For the Solo Practitioner

Assess all the proposal activities that have to be completed and determine whether or not it is realistic for one person to complete them all.

If you decide you can manage all the activities, set milestones for each one and stick to them. Conduct a daily meeting with yourself to assess how much progress you have made.

Even if you can create a realistic schedule for yourself, and write the entire proposal, consider engaging someone to be an external reviewer.

If possible, consider outsourcing other proposal tasks, especially administrative and clerical tasks, so you can focus on the solution and the writing.

of elapsed time, regardless of how hard people work. One example is getting quotes or formal bids from subcontractors. It takes the subcontractor a certain amount of time to get a quote approved and, although deadlines and reminders are essential, calling or emailing every hour is likely to backfire.

Brooks's Law, stipulates that, above a certain level of effort, adding more people to a task actually makes the task take longer to complete. This is counterintuitive, because, often, the first reaction when there is too much work and not enough time is to get more people and chop the work up into smaller pieces. One example of this is writing narrative proposal text. Creating narrative text is different from, and more difficult than, filling out a web-based form that calls for product specifications or other data points. Asking ten people to write five pages each of a 50-page proposal might make sense, depending on the writers and the type of text required. Asking 25 people to each write one paragraph of a five-page proposal clearly does not make sense.

Developing the schedule consists of four steps (see Figure 5.1). The final step, enforcing the schedule, is not a discrete activity but an ongoing responsibility for the proposal manager.

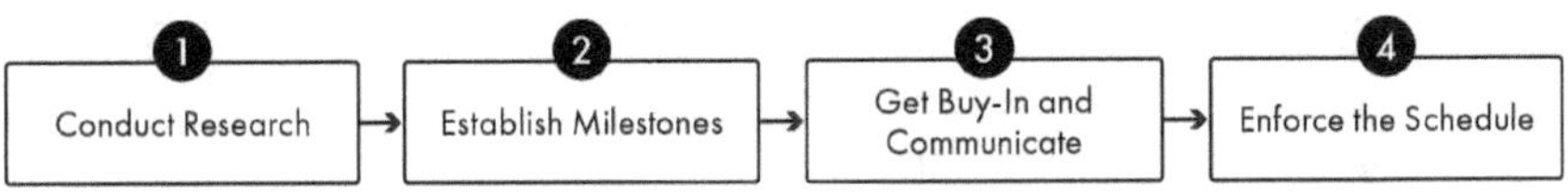

Figure 5.1 Steps in the Scheduling Process; It Is Important to Do Them in Sequence

Step 1: Research

Begin with research. You have to get data points if you want to build a schedule you can enforce. Make sure you have accurate information on the following:

- The due date and time for delivery (if the RFP is not clear, this is a critical question to ask during the period that questions are permitted). Because the opportunity, effort and expense attached to the proposal are irrevocably lost if it arrives even one minute late, no room for error exists;
- The exact place of delivery, including the name of the person who will confirm receipt. If it is a physical address, how long does it take to gain entry? Who will sign for the proposal? What advance arrangements do you have to make to be admitted? What hours of the day will someone be available to confirm receipt of the proposal by providing a signature? If it is an upload to a site or an email, log in to the site or send a

test email to make sure the address is valid. Determine whether or not a password is required to access the site and, if so, start the necessary steps to get one;

- How long it will take to deliver the proposal; add a margin of safety to allow for unpredictable events. Depending on the delivery logistics, that might mean two hours or five days. Courier services encounter delays in bad weather, and websites can be non-responsive if too many people are trying to log on at the same time. Every website is different, and geography varies, and no global rules exist to make sure that delivery occurs on time;
- How long it will take to format, edit and produce the proposal. This is an area where research is critical. Desktop publishers and editors are my best friends, and I honor and respect their work. I always defer to their estimates of how much time they will need for formatting and editing. They do not work for me; I work for them and do everything possible to make their job easier and give them the time they need. This means giving them a copy of the RFP as soon as possible and asking them for the most conservative estimate of the time they will require. Ideally, the desktop publisher is part of the team that analyzes the RFP and develops questions, so providing an estimate should not be too time-consuming. If the team is likely to include multiple writers who are not familiar with how to format text in the way required by the RFP, or if they are not used to writing formal prose, you will have to add more time for desktop publishers and editors. This is a balancing act, because more time for formatting typically comes at the expense of the time available for writing, and writers always want to steal that time back from the production schedule to continue to add content. Formatting and editing tasks that often trip people up include:
  - Adding headers and footers to spreadsheets;
  - Numbering figures and tables sequentially;
  - Checking to make sure references to figures and tables and all cross-references are correct;
  - Checking for style conventions (consistent use of upper or lower case, for example);
  - Acceptance or rejection of editor's suggested changes;
  - Removing all document properties;
  - Inserting cover page or cover;
  - Insertion of forms or contractual documents that are pre-formatted;

- How long it will take to check the proposal for accuracy and errors that an editor might not be able to catch (misspelled names or places, for example);

- The time required for the financial and legal parts of the proposal to be prepared, as well as interdependencies between the price or budget and the solution;
- What holidays or other paid time off for critical participants will affect the schedule. At this point, you might not know the names of everyone who is going to participate, but you can find this information out from the key players;
- Who, if anyone other than the proposal manager, should approve the proposal schedule. Exactly whom to consult will vary, depending on the size and structure of your organization. You cannot build a schedule by the consensus method, where everyone has to agree. But you also cannot build it in a vacuum without transparency and collaboration.

Yes, collecting all this information takes time. If you create a schedule without the right information, however, you will have to continually revise and adjust it. Not only does this inconvenience people who are fitting the proposal work in with many other commitments, it causes people to see all deadlines as temporary and subject to change. You have a much better chance of enforcing a schedule if you have consulted key people on the team and incorporated their input. Be sure you store important metrics, such as number of pages that your editor can finish per hour, so that you do not have to keep re-collecting the information for each proposal.

Step 2: Establish Milestones

As you establish milestones, consider two types of proposal activities. The first one is activities that are dependent on previous tasks. You cannot review a proposal before it is written. You cannot complete the editing or formatting of a proposal that is still being drafted. The second category is activities with a defined duration. It takes a certain amount of time to safely deliver a proposal. No matter how many efficiencies you introduce, you cannot change this. The same is true for proofreading, editing and desktop publishing. Filling solution gaps will take a certain amount of time, no matter what you do, because it takes time to get quotes from vendors or subcontractors or to modify an existing solution. Preparing questions on the RFP can only take so long because there is often (on US government procurements) a deadline for submitting questions very close to the release of the RFP.

The deadlines for this second category of activities are relatively easy to establish (although not necessarily to enforce) because they are externally imposed. On the other hand, documenting the solution and writing and revising text and graphics almost always expand to fill every minute of time available and so will require deadlines that you, as a proposal manager, develop and enforce.

Work backwards from the delivery date to establish how much time is available to write and review proposal content. Start with the due date and time, then move backwards in the calendar to allow enough time for the delivery, and then move further backwards to allow time for proofreading, editing, formatting and producing the proposal. As much as it is important to give the production staff enough time to do their work, the total time available is going to dictate how many days or hours you can budget for these activities. A two-week proposal is probably not going to get the same level of editing or attention to detail in formatting as a two-month proposal.

Once you have an estimate for formatting, editing and delivery, you can establish the date that contributors have to stop work, also referred to as "pens down," a milestone after which no one on the proposal team is allowed to make substantive changes to the text or graphics, except to correct serious omissions, inaccuracies or errors.

At this point, you will have the pillars of your schedule: the day and time that you have to stop all work and ship the proposal, and the day and time that the section owners have to turn their sections over for final editing and formatting. Those days and times are immutable. Others will depend on the specifics of your proposal activities and your judgment about how much time to allocate to them.

Establish deadlines for the eight fundamental activities discussed in this book (communication and daily proposal management occur throughout and do not get scheduled because they should be happening on a daily basis). Do not forget to budget time for analyzing the solicitation, creating a proposal outline, assembling a team and making assignments. The reason they constitute chapters in this book is that people typically schedule almost no time for them and assume them into existence. In a perfect world, the eight fundamental steps occur sequentially. In the real world, several of them overlap and often happen simultaneously.

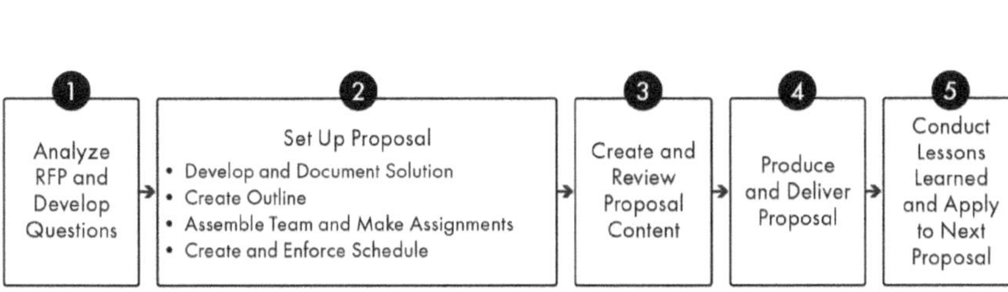

Figure 5.2 Steps in the Proposal Process – a Mix of Sequential and Simultaneous Activities

Determine how much time is left between the solution lock and the pens-down milestone and then establish interim deadlines for completion and review of the proposal sections. Make sure there are short intervals so that section owners get a break and reviewers can comment on the document and provide suggestions to make it stronger. No hard and fast rule exists to tell you how many proposal reviews you should have, when they should occur or how much time to give section owners to develop content. This will depend on the quality of the writing, the maturity and complexity of the solution and the quality of the reviewers. Even if the time available for creating and reviewing proposal content is short, and only one person is designated as a reviewer, it is still important to break the time up into discrete work phases. If you have a lot of time to work with, beware! Giving people three weeks to perform a task that could be accomplished in a week does not mean that it will be done on time. (It is the corollary to my rule about airline travel: when you have five hours in between flights, that is when you miss your plane.) No contributor should work independently, without checkpoints, progress reports or reviews, for longer than a week.

As you are establishing the deadlines for writing and reviewing, determine whether or not work on some proposal sections can begin before the solution is locked down. For example, can someone start preparing resumes? Can someone start descriptions of previous contracts or projects? Whether or not this is possible depends on the maturity of the solution. A mature solution makes it easy to begin some sections early. But, if you start those sections early and then a group of engineers emerges with a brilliant new methodology or software application, it could change every section of the proposal, including the resumes and the past performance. Asking people to re-do something they have already done is demoralizing and it undercuts the perception of the proposal manager as someone competent and in charge.

Next, document the detailed steps for editing, proofreading, formatting and physical production and delivery, even down to the hour, if you can. You should have this to defend your schedule if you encounter opposition. I do not share this with the team, but I always have it ready, because, invariably, someone on the team wants to extend that final pens-down date and time. A production schedule for a 50-page proposal with only a CD, and no hard copy for delivery, might look something like Table 5.1.

Include in your schedule time to prepare and conduct a kick-off meeting. In an ideal world, this is where everyone on the team agrees on all roles and responsibilities, the solution, the schedule, the outline and the review process. Once you have handled the fundamentals, add the other activities not discussed here: pricing and business case reviews, communication

Table 5.1 Sample Production Schedule

Prior to Monday morning		*Desktop publisher checks CD burner* *Desktop publisher creates shipping label, airbill and receipt for proposal manager approval* *Proposal manager confirms pick-up or delivery time for courier service or post office*
Monday	8:00 am	Editor has configuration control and makes edits
Tuesday	8:00 am	Section owners accept or reject editor changes
Tuesday	10:00 am	Desktop publisher formats document
Tuesday	3:00 pm	Desktop publisher prints or publishes proof copy
Tuesday	5:00 pm	Desktop publisher addresses any formatting issues or questions
Wednesday	8:00 am	Desktop publisher prints second proof copy
Wednesday	10:00 am	Proposal manager reviews proof copy ("white glove")
Wednesday	11:00 am	Desktop publisher addresses any remaining issues
Wednesday	1:00 pm	Desktop publisher burns first CD and checks
Wednesday	2:00 pm	Desktop publisher burns remaining five CDs
Wednesday	4:00 pm	Proposal manager checks all CDs
Wednesday	5:30 pm	Proposal coordinator wraps and seals CDs and delivers to courier service or post office

and negotiation with subcontractors and vendors, revising graphics and completing all administrative proposal artifacts such as forms and tables, adding signatures where necessary.

Typically, half the time available to prepare a proposal goes to the planning at the beginning (establishing a schedule, analyzing the RFP, clarifying the solution) and the formatting, production and delivery at the end. This is a textbook rule and has been a question on the APMP exam for Foundation certification. However, standard percentages are just the departure point for building a schedule. Many proposals have unique formatting or production requirements, holidays and time off for staff, difficult delivery instructions or other characteristics that will make one phase take proportionately longer.

Complicated proposal graphics, illustrations or photographs require time in the schedule as well as expertise. Although the tools are available to almost anyone who has a laptop, a less-than-professional job can undermine creditability. Yet engaging a professional adds expense as well as time. This is a tradeoff that the proposal manager should discuss early on with the capture manager or other senior executive.

Resist the temptation to pad the schedule. If a section has to be done by noon on Tuesday to meet the production deadlines, do not tell the writer to finish by Friday evening. This undermines the proposal manager's credibility. Once people find out that the schedule has extra time built in, they will assume that the rest of the deadlines are also not the real ones and give themselves extra time. They might also discount the proposal manager's other assignments and decisions. It pays to be honest with the team about the realities of the schedule, and the result is usually increased respect for the proposal manager's authority. By the same token, once you set a deadline, do not tell contributors that you actually need them to be done earlier. Once there is a deadline, people make plans and organize their time. Failing to respect that undermines trust.

"She said it is due Thursday, but I know she doesn't really need it until next Tuesday ... and I have to get back to my day job."

Finally, make sure that any proposal deadlines that you own as proposal manager, such as distribution of the proposal outline, are ones that you can meet. It will be very difficult to get others to keep to your schedule if you miss your own deadlines.

Step 3: Get Buy-In and Communicate the Schedule

Before you communicate the schedule, decide how to enforce the milestones in the schedule. It is very rare for a proposal manager to have all the authority needed to enforce the schedule. Any proposal team that includes more than a few people has one person who cannot, or will not, meet deadlines. Applying pressure to meet a deadline on someone who outranks you is not easy; this is why it is almost never a good idea to assign ownership of a proposal section to a senior executive. Find out early on who is going to provide support when deadlines slip and you have to escalate. Otherwise, the proposal manager is accountable for a result with no ability to control the steps that will bring about the result. Likewise, find out if there is someone who has the authority to change the schedule later in the process and get that person's buy-in early.

Then, communicate the schedule to everyone on the team at a kick-off meeting. It is not always necessary to share every interim deadline, but, sometimes, it is helpful for convincing skeptics who always think that some phases, such as editing, can be compressed. If you have done your research and your homework, you can communicate the milestones with confidence and with data to back you up.

I like to prepare the schedule in a calendar format, because that is how we perceive time and that is how it is easiest to understand.

Explain the realities of proposal editing, formatting and delivery. The widespread use of desktop applications such as MS Word and MS PowerPoint make it easy for writers and subject matter experts to think that it takes no time to incorporate minor changes, such as adding a sentence here or an image there at the last minute. Technically, the keystrokes take very little time. However, these changes often have implications for other pages or sections of the proposal. Adding a new resume often means changing the way the proposal is priced. Adding one line to a page can throw off the formatting of all the subsequent pages and result in a proposal that exceeds the permitted page length. Moreover, these last-minute additions often have embedded errors that are difficult to catch because there is no time left for another round of proofreading and fact checking.

Step 4: Enforce the Schedule

Once the schedule is final, resist the temptation to adjust it unless there is a very compelling reason, such as a change in the due date. The first time the schedule slips, contributors tend to think that future deadlines will also slip, and it becomes very difficult to enforce the discipline needed to complete the proposal on time.

The only way to know whether or not you are staying on schedule is to check progress towards milestones daily, either in a team meeting or through communication with individual contributors. High-performing teams, whether they are proposal teams or not, use a daily stand-up, which consists of a short status call in which everyone who owns a deliverable reports progress in specific terms. This is also a chance to identify roadblocks and share new information. The status call is best when it is short (I prefer a maximum of 15 minutes) and when it includes everyone, not just owners, but those in support roles too.

Invariably, people push back on this idea, preferring to work at their own pace, minimize meetings and use the time for their own priorities. I have never seen a proposal without a daily call succeed. It does not matter whether the proposal lasts a week or a year. If you keep the calls brief, people get used to the rhythm and attend, and, if there is not much to say, you can end the call early.

Proposal section owners should share their drafts daily, whether on a shared collaborative workspace, such as SharePoint, or on a physical proposal wall. Participants push back on this demand also. But it is a best practice for a reason. Without visibility of daily progress, the proposal manager has no way of knowing whether the right people have been assigned. Because you will almost certainly encounter resistance when enforcing this rule, get support for this from someone senior in the company who can help enforce it if necessary.

Silence is not golden. Silence invariably indicates an issue. Whenever possible, visit contributors in their workplace. If you are not co-located, request a video call. Seeing someone's surroundings can be an excellent clue.

When someone does not meet a deadline or fails to share work in progress, the first step is to perform a root cause analysis to determine the source of the problem. In the case of a writer, the reason is often that the person does not know what to write or how to write it. It can be difficult to uncover this reason because people do not typically want to admit that they do not know – they think everyone else knows, and they should know, too. Ironically, at some point everyone is in the position of not knowing, because proposal writing is not something taught at school, and everyone has a first time. Other possibilities exist as well. It could be that the individual is dealing with a family or personal emergency that was not foreseeable when the schedule was established. The writer might have too many other commitments to be able to complete the proposal work on time and no ability to delegate other assignments and make the proposal a priority. The writer might be someone who always finished papers in college in the middle of the night before they were due. The appropriate step for the proposal manager is going to be very different depending on which of the situations pertains.

When the proposal manager does not have the authority to address the underlying cause of the delay, escalation is essential. Everyone in an organization reports to someone. Although going above someone's head is an intimidating prospect for many, and particularly for first-time proposal managers, failing to escalate is a disservice to others on the team who are working hard to meet deadlines and finish the proposal on time.

Spotting non-performers early is essential to staying on schedule. When someone does not deliver on time, the process of figuring out why and taking corrective action itself takes time, possibly delaying the schedule even further. If you have done your homework, you will be prepared for this eventuality.

Conclusion

Developing and enforcing a schedule requires attention to detail and vigilance. Take the time to think carefully about interim deadlines and how best to get buy-in and support. Spotting problems early and escalating them quickly are essential, as is honest communication with the team.

Chapter 6

Creating Proposal Content

Definition

This activity consists of creating and inserting text and, where appropriate, charts, images, photographs or tables, following the structure of the outline (see Chapter 3) already created. The type of content needed for each proposal section or volume can vary greatly, from material that has to conform to very specific rules, formatting and length to material that bidders can organize any way they see fit. The content might be highly technical or extremely theoretical or it might be straightforward descriptions of the features of a system or methodology.

Why Is it Important?

If you do not have the right content, you will not be successful in winning the contract, grant or award. "Right" means that the content is: (1.) compliant with the instructions and (2.) compelling in demonstrating that your organization is the right one to do the job or provide the system or product, based on the information from the RFP as to how the content will be evaluated.

Challenges

There are challenges both for the proposal manager and for the writers. Few proposal managers have enough subject matter knowledge to know whether each section owner is progressing at the right pace to finish the work on schedule. Yet they are accountable for the results. Words on a page alone do not necessarily constitute progress. An additional difficulty for the proposal manager is a reluctance to send reminders (and make yourself something of a pest) to more senior professionals and subject matter experts who might take offense, complain or worse. There are polite ways to do this, but it is best to expect that you will not always be the most popular person on the proposal team.

DOI: 10.4324/9781003581475-7

For the writers, whether they are subject matter experts or proposal managers, no one formula exists for creating compliant, compelling text for each proposal section. Each section and each RFP pose unique challenges. The executive summary requires a different kind of writing from the quality control plan, the resumes, the pricing assumptions or the technical approach. Even if you are an experienced proposal writer or subject matter expert, you cannot simply copy what you wrote last time or apply the same process. Furthermore, the time available in the proposal schedule to create content is short, and the deadlines are real. Writers are often juggling multiple assignments in addition to the proposal, which only increases the time pressure. Writing compelling proposal content or revising previous content to make it relevant requires concentration and focus for sustained periods of time. It is very difficult to complete a proposal section by working on it for 15 minutes here and there throughout the day. Big blocks of time and serious attention are out of reach for many, given the pull of conflicting commitments and the lure of digital devices. An additional challenge is the fact that creating compliant content that satisfies the RFP requirements requires a different type of thinking from creating compelling content that makes a convincing case for your services or product. Both are critical, and few people can do both at the same time.

When Does it Happen?

This step occurs after you have created an outline, assembled a team and documented your solution. It is possible to start some proposal sections earlier, if you are confident that the solution is stable. For example, if the RFP calls for examples of your previous contracts or grants, someone on the team can begin to write up your project descriptions shortly after you receive the RFP, possibly before the solution team has met. Likewise, if you know who is going to be the project or program manager, you can begin preparing resumes earlier. I am always cautious about this because, until the solution is documented and locked down, even a small tweak can result in changes across all the proposal sections, including the resumes and the past performance. It is a balancing act for the proposal manager to decide whether it is worth the risk that some of the early work will require revisions or even overhaul.

Who Owns it?

The proposal manager is ultimately accountable for making sure the right content is in the proposal. Others are responsible for creating, reviewing and revising the content; the proposal manager tracks content development and provides support and direction to writers. In practice, proposal managers often write and rewrite paragraphs and sometimes pages or even sections, usually non-technical ones such as resumes or descriptions of previous experience, especially if the deadline is approaching and the person assigned to the section is struggling to create the right content.

Steps in the Process

The steps here can be used by writers and by proposal managers who become writers during the proposal process. For short sections that are governed by specific instructions, writers do not require much direction beyond the RFP language. The steps here are best used for creating narrative text. Some examples include:

- Description of the product or service;
- Explanation of a methodology or process;
- Explanation of tasks and subtasks you will be performing;
- Description of the qualifications of the people on the project and their tasks;
- Explanation of the outcome or results from the project;
- Justification of the price or budget;
- Description of similar contracts or projects your company has executed;
- Explanation of any assumptions or conditions.

Many RFPs, particularly notifications for grant proposals, include only basic instructions for certain sections. For example, one recent US government RFP contained the following instructions for a 25-page section: "Describe how you will manage the project and make sure all resources are available when needed." How to organize and explain the management approach was at the discretion of the bidder. These can be challenging assignments even for experienced proposal professionals because the right approach to developing this content is not immediately obvious, and opinions will differ as to which one is best.

The steps here can be used for any narrative proposal section. If you are the sole writer for all proposal sections, follow the steps in order to avoid unnecessary revisions and rewriting. If you are leading a team of writers, keep these ideas in your back pocket until you can gauge the writing skills of your team. It is not always a good idea to force a specific writing process. Subject matter experts and proposal writers might have their own approach; if they follow instructions, meet deadlines and create compelling content, they probably do not need a lot of direction. But, if they do not know where to start, the process below offers some structure and some hints that will make the writers more productive. The writers who admit their inexperience or inability to move forward are easier to manage than the ones who are convinced they are good writers and are not. Either way, your job as a proposal manager is to support the writers by offering feedback, finding data points and helping to organize proposal sections when the RFP is unclear or contradictory.

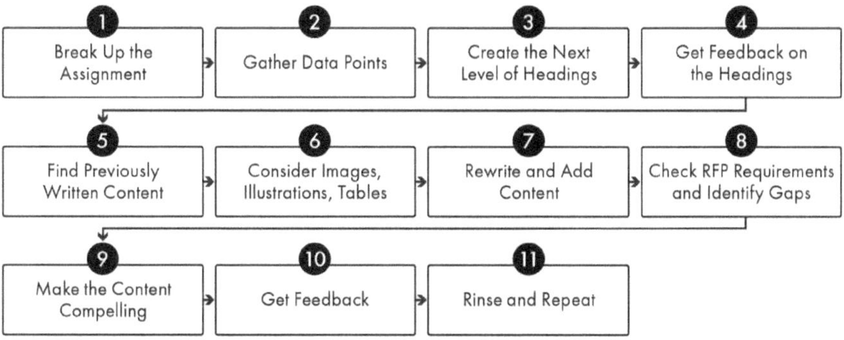

Figure 6.1 Steps to Create Content; Repeat the Cycle as Many Times as Possible Given the Proposal Deadlines

Step 1: Break the Assignment into Pieces and Finish the First Piece

This is the hardest step for many subject matter experts who receive proposal writing assignments. Writing 20 or 30 pages seems like an overwhelming task, and it can be. But, if you set aside time to assemble and review the proposal outline, the solution documentation and any previous proposals or marketing material that is relevant to the section you are writing, you have taken the first step, and the momentum will carry you forward. Setting specific and realistic goals you can accomplish in a discrete period of time results in greater productivity than tackling a large job all at once. Although it is true that writing (good writing, anyway) cannot be sandwiched in or compressed into tiny increments, it is also a mistake for most people to plan to create content for hours at a time. If this is the way you write, congratulations. For the rest of us, as I learned in working on this book manuscript, serious attention for 30–40 minutes, followed by a mental or physical break, a walk around the block, a cup of tea, is much more productive than chaining myself to my desk for a four-hour stretch. Likewise, for most people, the morning hours are more productive than late nights. Invariably, people who write a lot have routines and rituals that get them going. For me, it is reading short extracts from my favorite essays and letters. Some people listen to a particular piece of music. Some people meditate to clear their minds. There is no one right answer.

Step 2: Gather the Data Points

If completing the section requires data points that are not in the solution documentation, such as the qualifications of the staff or examples of previous use of the methodology being proposed, take time to do the research and gather these together before doing anything else. Sometimes, there is a long lead time for the research, and, if you leave it until the end, you might run out of time. Data that should be easy to find, in both small organizations and large ones, are often not.

Step 3: Create the Next Level of Headings

Every proposal section has a structure. Before you start writing text, make sure you have the compliance-driven headings described in Chapter 3. Do not confuse the term "heading" with "header." A heading is a label for one or more paragraphs of text; a header is the text that appears in the top margin of the page, such as the page number, the date and the company name. Reread the steps in the outline process in Chapter 3 so that you are clear on which headings are compliance-driven, and should not be changed, and which ones are author-driven. Lower-level or subordinate headings chosen by the writer break the topic into its component parts, and it is good to have as many levels as practical, given the page count for the section you are writing. These headings are helpful both to the writer and to the reader. For the reader, they label and telegraph the main points and the flow. For writers, it is typically easier to create a sentence fragment, which is what a heading is, than it is to craft full paragraphs of text. Creating headings forces you to think through your content and plan it before you write. Adding headings will keep you focused on what you consider essential about your approach. If author-driven, lower-level headings exist already, break the topic down further into smaller and smaller pieces.

For some people, it helps to put each topic on a sticky note and move the notes around on the wall until the content is organized in a logical way. Do not worry how many levels of headings you create. If you create three or four levels of headings, some of them might be eliminated in a later draft, but they are helpful now.

How long this step takes and how you go about it is going to depend a great deal on the proposal outline created by the proposal manager and the number of pages in the section you are working on. Two examples illustrate how to think about outlining the section. Example 1 is based on a very prescriptive RFP with tight page limits, where all the headings in the outline are dictated by the RFP.

Example 1

Corporate Experience (2-page limit)

1.0 Experience Using EastWind Software

1.1 Start and End Date of Contract
1.2 Customer Point of Contact
1.3 Description of Work Performed

2.0 Experience Applying Software to Construction Scheduling

2.1 Start and End Date of Contract
2.2 Customer Point of Contact
2.3 Description of Work Performed

3.0 Experience Managing Subcontractors

3.1 Start and End Date of Contract
3.2 Customer Point of Contact
3.3 Description of Work Performed

You will not have to create any subheadings below the ones already in the outline for the dates and points of contact, because they are one-line data points. Filling in these fields is a fact-finding exercise and not a difficult writing job. The only place you would probably want additional headings is under "Description of the Work" for each contract, and, even there, two or three headings are probably plenty, because with the page constraints, it is best to not use too many headings. In this scenario, the lower-level, writer-driven headings you might add are indicated in italics.

Corporate Experience

1. Experience Using EastWind Software

1.1 Start and End Date of Contract
1.2 Customer Point of Contact
1.3 Description of Work

1.3.1 How we configured the software
1.3.2 How we tested the software

1.3.3 How we implemented the software
1.3.4 Our results

2.0 Experience Applying Software to Construction Scheduling

2.1 Start and End Date of Contract
2.2 Customer Point of Contact
2.3 Description of Work Performed

2.3.1 What was the construction project?
2.3.2 What were the challenges?
2.3.3 How did we modify the software?
2.3.4 Our results

3.0 Experience Managing Subcontractors

3.1 Start and End Date of Contract
3.2 Customer Point of Contact
3.3 Description of Work Performed

3.3.1 Number of subcontracts
3.3.2 Subcontractor communication and coordination
3.3.3 Subcontractor performance results

You have now created 11 mini writing assignments, each one of which is likely to be only a few sentences at most.

Example 2 is quite different. In this example, the proposal manager has annotated the outline with the instructions from the RFP.

Example 2: Technical Approach

(40-page limit; describe in detail the methodology to be used in analyzing the data from each of the four main sources)

1. Geographic Data
2. Demographic Data
3. Financial Data
4. Historical Data

This example calls for conceptual thinking. The text under each major heading is likely to be ten pages. This requires making some decisions.

Do you want to describe the methodology as a chronology? Do you want to focus on one process or offer a menu of possibilities? Do you want to discuss the challenges inherent in each type of data? Are all the sources equally important or should you spend more pages on some than others? Do you want to provide examples of other data sets you have analyzed?

When creating headings, speed is important, and done is better than perfect. Try a number of different ways of organizing the material and see which one makes the most sense. Often, your first instinct is the best one, and overthinking results in adding unnecessary complexity. Work fast. The same people who excelled in school and treat proposal assignments like homework often have an inner critic that is editing as they write. Just get your thoughts down quickly and you can edit later, after you get some distance from your work and get some feedback. The more headings you create, the more mini writing assignments you will have, and the easier it will be to complete each one.

As you do this step, pay attention to parallel structure, as explained in Chapter 3. The task of writing this book got much easier as soon as I found a common structure that I could use to organize each chapter. A consistent structure makes the document easier to read and understand and much easier to write. For example, if you have to discuss a methodology for six separate tasks, it is best to organize your thoughts in a similar way for each task, perhaps as in the box.

Task One: Requirements Definition

- Introduction
- Inputs
- Outputs
- Specific Steps in the Process
- Experience Conducting Similar Tasks
- Results Achieved Using the Process

Task Two: Discovery

- Introduction
- Inputs
- Outputs
- Specific Steps in the Process
- Experience Conducting Similar Tasks
- Results Achieved Using the Process

Step 4: Get Feedback on Your Headings

Once you have inserted headings, ask a colleague or the proposal manager to comment on your headings. If you are a proposal manager, encourage writers and section owners to share their work early and often. Getting feedback now is critical, because it is much easier to reorganize or change headings than it is to rewrite or reorganize large chunks of text.

In Example 2 above, opinions probably differ as to the best way to organize each of the subsections, and the time to get additional input is before you spend several days or weeks writing the 25 pages, not after. Even in Example 1, which is much more straightforward, it is good to get feedback as a form of sanity check.

Step 5: Find Previously Created Content Relevant to Your Headings

Pick one small section of the proposal as a departure point. This is going to be your "proof of concept." In the outline above, you might want to start with Section 1.3.1, "How We Configured the Software." Gather together previous proposals, papers, brochures and solution documentation that relate to the software configuration and, very selectively, paste in content that relates directly to the work that you are proposing, tailoring each sentence to make it applicable. It is always easier to start with what already exists. "Good artists copy; great artists steal." The proposal management literature is full of admonitions about using "boilerplate," and for good reason. Copying and pasting large chunks of text from a previous proposal carries the risk that you will be proposing the wrong solution and it will be obvious to the reader that you are simply regurgitating an old proposal. However, the reality is that almost no one writes a proposal entirely from scratch. The way out of this contradiction is to use previous material very deliberately and judiciously. It is not easy but, for most people, it is easier than starting with a blank page. New content always draws on what was created previously, either implicitly or explicitly. As an example, this book, I hope, presents a new way of thinking about proposal management, but it also draws heavily on articles I have written and talks I have given on the same topic.

This step serves another purpose. If you cannot find any material relevant to your section, if there is no solution documentation and there are no previous proposal sections, you have identified a red flag. If the solution team did not think through the details and document them, your company is taking a risk in proposing something you have never done before and possibly do not really know how to do. It is time to escalate to the proposal manager or a senior executive before trying to write something from thin air.

Step 6: Consider Images, Illustrations, Tables

Before editing previous text or inserting new text, think through the best way to present the information with something other than multiple paragraphs of text. If there are a lot of data, tables are often more effective than narrative alone and they break up the page, giving the reader more white space. Likewise, photographs can be helpful in conveying the intangibles, but make sure they are relevant and high quality. Consider using a flow chart to describe a process rather than words alone. If you have trouble identifying a diagram or chart, check to see if the topic in your section falls into one of these categories:

- Before versus after. Are you describing a process followed by a result?
- Bridge to the future. Are you describing the transition to a better, future state?
- Layout. Are you describing a physical or geographic location?
- System. Are you describing something with multiple components that fit together?
- Loop. Are you describing an iterative process?
- Hierarchy. Are you describing relationships between people or ideas in a way that shows their levels or significance?

Writers, particularly experts in highly technical fields, often struggle creating graphics or images. Many tools and resources exist to help generate ideas.[1] The effective use of graphics in proposals is the topic of a book unto itself.[2] Often, time is limited, and simpler is better, because creating a proposal graphic from scratch will easily eat up hours that you probably do not have. Sometimes, a graphic from a previous proposal can work (with revisions). Even the use of an icon to represent a concept gives the reader a break from reading text. If you want to emphasize timeliness, for example, you can insert a small icon of an alarm clock each time you refer to the schedule. Icons work best when you use them consistently throughout the proposal. It does not make sense to use them only once. If you cannot think of anything, move on and ask other to help you define graphics to support the content. Consider engaging a professional who understands page layout and reader preferences to work with you on illustrations or photos unless you have those skills. The investment will pay back many times over because it will enable the writers to focus on the content. Otherwise, the appearance of the document takes on a life of its own and can quickly derail the proposal schedule.

Regardless of who prepares the graphic, find out how the customer will be reviewing the proposal. If it is an electronic review, the software used to support the reviewer might not be able to identify a graphical representation of your text. For this reason, unless you know what software will be used, the safe route is to have graphics and illustrations that repeat what is in your text and not rely on them to tell a complete story.

Step 7: Rewrite and Add Content

Once you have inserted content and identified tables and graphics, tailor the material further to make sure it is relevant to the RFP. Add text where you have gaps or create placeholders with yellow highlighting if you do not know or cannot find the content. Make sure there is a logical flow from one sentence to the next. Make sure the tense is consistent (typically either present or future, unless you are describing previous experience). Whenever possible, put the main point of each paragraph at the beginning, not the end, of the paragraph. If you are writing about a topic that relates directly to other proposal sections, make a note of the relationship, but do not get distracted by trying to tie everything together. Treat this one section as if it were independent of the rest of the proposal. You can insert cross-references and look at other relevant proposal sections later.

Insert specifics and examples wherever you can. Generalizations do not convey competence. Consider these two examples:

1 We have a robust quality control program that enables us to keep all our customers satisfied.
2 We monitor every 10th phone call and rate it for courtesy, length, problem resolution and closure. Since introducing this monitoring system, our customer satisfaction rate increased from 40% to 85%.

Someone with no knowledge or expertise could write the first example, but only someone with industry-specific competence could write the second one.

If you make an assertion, be prepared to prove it with statistics, photos, customer testimonials or other data. If you cannot find the data, insert a placeholder and get help from others to fill the gap.

As you write, answer the basic journalism questions of who, how, when, where and why. Although proposal text has to be directly relevant and traceable to the RFP requirements, it is essential to go beyond repeating or paraphrasing them. In fact, some US government solicitations include statements such as "proposals that merely restate the requirements will not be considered acceptable." Proposal writers often fail to explain the "how" of the solution and write too many words about the "what." The reason for this is either that the writer does not know the details of the solution or that the solution team itself has not worked through the specific steps or processes. It is the job of the writer to get as many answers as possible, and the job of the proposal manager to support the writer in requesting more detail.

Create transition sentences to link the paragraphs together. Focus on following the instructions at this stage, and not on selling the solution. Once you have a complete draft, you can add content that conveys why your company is the best choice, why your competitors will not be able to do the job and how your product or service outshines all the others. Right now, it is important to put all the relevant facts and concepts into the section.

Beware of trying to make the prose interesting. At this stage, proposal sections will likely be dry and uninteresting, and that is fine. You are aiming for accuracy and completeness. You can introduce text that will make it compelling in a later step.

Step 8: Check RFP Requirements and Identify Gaps

In a perfect world, each writer receives a worksheet from the proposal manager that includes all the relevant RFP instructions and requirements. It might look something like the sidebar.

In the real world, proposal managers rarely have time to spoon-feed writers. It falls to the writer to check the RFP, and then check it again, to make sure that the section is complete. If the RFP asks for the color, weight and dimensions of the product, make sure you have all three. If a few details are missing, you can insert them later (as long as you have a way of keeping track of them). But, if your section is full of placeholders, this is a sign that you do not have the expertise or the information you need to complete the section, and it is critical to discuss this with the proposal manager as soon as you can.

Writer's Instructions

Section #: 2.3

Section Title: Customer Service

Page Limit: 3

Section Due Date: August 12

Instructions from RFP: Describe plans, methods, and mindset for defining, addressing, anticipating and serving customers.

Evaluation Criteria from RFP: Bidders will be evaluated for the realism and quality of their customer service approach.

Requirements from the RFP:

1.7.12 Develop, submit to the Department and

implement a Customer Service Resolution Plan within 30 days of the Contract start date.

1.7.13 Maintain a Customer Service Log detailing concerns, requests and the resolution of the items contained in the log.

Step 9: Revise and Add Content to Make the Sections Compelling

Once you have populated all the sections and made a note of the data points or concepts that are missing – and you have created a plan to fill these gaps – read through the section looking for areas where you can highlight unique features of your offering and how they will benefit the customer. Look for ways you can distinguish your solution from the competitors' solutions in ways that will resonate with the customer.

Proposal courses and books always emphasize, for good reason, the importance of customizing proposal content to meet customer preferences. For example, a lower price might not be important to a customer who cares more about quality or security or on-time delivery. If you do not have a good understanding of what the customer values, it is extremely difficult to write compelling prose. For a proposal manager, this can pose a challenge. Often, the most significant insights about customer preferences are in someone's head and not in customer relation management software or capture plans. Transferring the knowledge acquired about an opportunity over time can be difficult once a solicitation arrives and the pressure of deadlines begins. In other instances, the information about the customer might be outdated or inaccurate.

There are times when there simply is not any information to help you understand how to address customer concerns. It is very common for this to happen when responding to US federal government RFPs because most government agencies do not reveal the names or positions of the people who will be evaluating the proposal. If you are in this situation, first, ask the capture manager, senior executive or business development manager to provide insight; this is their job. Often, the people who have the customer knowledge have never documented it and assume everyone else knows what they know. If you cannot get any insights from the business development or capture executives, conduct your own research. Many organizations publish mission statements, annual reports, budgets, priorities and press releases about recent developments. These sources can all help you customize your proposal section.

If you are bidding for a contract with a commercial customer, your company is likely to have more opportunities to find out about likes and dislikes. Keep asking the business development team to provide updated customer information and, if you are preparing a proposal for a foundation grant, try to speak directly with the program officer. They are often available to speak with applicants and provide important guidance.

Once you know what is important to the customer, you can use one of the many proposal techniques described in the APMP *Body of Knowledge* as well as proposal books and articles.[3] The most common ones are in Table 6.1. Not all are useful for every proposal, and each opportunity is unique. What is important is to apply these techniques once you have created content for each proposal heading that is complete, accurate and in conformance with the RFP requirements.

Table 6.1 Common Proposal Techniques

Value proposition	A statement that quantifies how your solution will improve outcomes for your customer
Feature	A description of one aspect of your solution, such as scale, unique functionality, technical performance, price
Benefit	A statement explaining the positive results of your solution for your customer (results that you are sure the customer will recognize as positive)
Ghosting	A statement about your solution that implies a comparison with your competition (for example, if you know your competitor has high personnel turnover, you can emphasize your high retention rate)
Strength	For US federal government proposals, a unique aspect of your solution that exceeds the RFP requirement in a way that the customer values, minimizes cost or risk, or contributes to mission success
Discriminator	A unique aspect of your solution that other bidders will not be proposing
Win theme	A one- or two-sentence summary of a proposal section that emphasizes the value proposition. Win themes are hard to create for proposals with a lot of details that do not lend themselves to simplification

Once you have customized the section to reflect customer knowledge, insert cross-references if one part of your section relates to another, or if your section relates directly to an assignment given to another writer. This is also a good time to check for consistent use of terminology, as well as spelling and grammar errors.

Step 10: Get Feedback

Identify someone who can provide feedback on the section. This is not the same as the formal review process described in Chapter 7 (the blue, pink, red and gold team reviews). This is an informal review by a non-expert. It might be a subject matter expert, the proposal manager, a business development manager, a colleague or a senior executive. It is important to find someone who can give you constructive feedback, someone who can use verbs rather than adjectives. Comments such as "this is terrible" or "this is awkward" are not actionable. Ask for comments that start with verbs: "add the results of our XYZ contract" or "change the order of the sentences in this paragraph so that they are consistent with the chronology" or "insert a flow chart to describe the process."

This step is almost as hard for some people as getting started. The more educated and accomplished the professional, the more likely they do not want to share their work until they think it is "perfect." Often, these professionals seem to behave as though they were still in school and treat the proposal assignment like a homework assignment that they have to complete on their own, and where the only acceptable grade is an "A." The proposal manager's job is to persuade section owners that the assignment is not connected to a promotion or a raise. Moreover, in Proposal Land, there is no such thing as an "A." There is no "perfect." It is always possible to improve until the time runs out.

Professional writers learn to create distance between themselves and their work early in their careers. They share their work in progress because they know that early feedback will save time and energy. If you apply the feedback you get on one small piece of the proposal to the subsequent sections, you avoid lengthy and painful revisions later on.

Ask your colleague to review this initial section for clarity and completeness, and nothing else.

For the Solo Practitioner

This activity is easier for you because you do not need to manage multiple writers and make sure they stay on schedule.

Decide on a discrete period of time for creating content. Isolate this from other administrative tasks (budget, legal or contractual issues).

Find someone in your network who can give you feedback on your content. It might mean calling in a favor or paying someone to be your sounding board. It will be worth it.

A fresh pair of eyes will identify potential errors that you, as the writer, are blind to. Most people do not realize the kinds of tricks our eyes play on us, but examples are everywhere. Take an online proofreading test to see for yourself how many errors you regularly ignore.

If your proposal has sections that have identical formatting, such as multiple resumes, task areas or descriptions of previous work, get feedback on the first resume and the first past performance description before you create content for all of them. Revise based on the feedback and then get consensus from others that the first one will create the standard for the others. Once there is one good example, you can achieve consistency across all the resumes or project descriptions and avoid extensive revisions of all of them.

Step 11: Rinse and Repeat

Examine the feedback and revise accordingly. You might not be able to incorporate all the suggestions you receive. Or, you might have to find additional people to review your section if you do not get meaningful feedback. Repeat the cycle as many times as the schedule permits. Get used to sharing work in progress, even if it feels uncomfortable at first.

"I'm still polishing it.
It's mostly written but it needs a little more work."

Conclusion

If you as a writer cannot follow these steps, or if you are managing writers who are not delivering content, it is likely that there is an underlying issue with the writing assignment itself, the solution, the outline or all three. Incomplete information can result in the wrong writer being assigned to a section. Not everyone will admit that they are encountering difficulties; the typical response is to report progress and ask for more time. In addition, assigning someone to write a section for which there is virtually no content is, unfortunately, a common practice. Creating proposal text out of thin air is a hopeless proposition! Sometimes, people get stuck for other reasons. They cannot figure out a logical flow. They cannot organize their thoughts. They do not understand how their section relates to other sections. If someone is stuck, the proposal manager is the person who is supposed to get them un-stuck. The proposal manager might have to engage a subject matter expert, or a technical writer, or a graphic artist, or a business development executive. Sometimes, people can express their ideas verbally but have trouble writing them down, and the transcript of a taped interview can get them back on track. But everyone needs support during the writing process, even if it is just words of encouragement.

Notes

1 Dan Roam, *The Back of the Napkin: Solving Problems and Selling Ideas with Pictures*, Portfolio/Penguin, 2008; Corey Sommers and David Jenkins, *Whiteboard Selling: Empowering Sales through Visuals*, Wiley, 2013; Nancy Duarte, *Resonate: Present Visual Stories That Transform Audiences*, Wiley, 2010, and *Data Stories: Explain Data and Inspire Action through Story*, Ideapress, 2019; Nora Herting and Heather Willems, *Draw Your Big Idea: The Ultimate Creativity Tool for Turning Thoughts into Actions and Dreams into Reality!* Chronicle Books, 2016.

2 Mike Parkinson, *Do-It-Yourself Billion Dollar Graphics: 3 Fast and Easy Steps to Turn Your Text and Ideas into Graphics That Sell*, Peppermill Press, 2007, http://billiondollargraphics.com/ebook; http://www.billiondollargraphics.com/GCS.pdf; http://billiondollargraphics.com/build-a-graphic.

3 Larry Newman, *Shipley Proposal Guide 4.1*, Perfect Paperback, 2017; Bob Lohfeld, *10 Steps to Creating High Scoring Proposals*, Lohfeld Consulting Group, 2017.

Chapter 7

Proposal Reviews

Definition

Every proposal, whether it is a single-screen online form or a multi-volume document with hundreds of pages, benefits from a review. A review is a critique by someone with a fresh set of eyes. In the same way that athletic teams have coaches, writers and graphic artists need constructive feedback to make sure the proposal is complete, accurate and compelling. The longer and the more complex the document, the greater the need for a review. In large organizations, proposals undergo multiple reviews as the document matures.

A review occurs when one or more people who have not been involved in creating proposal content read the proposal document and provide feedback on how to improve it. In a perfect world, reviewers are able to simulate the likely reaction of the customers who will be evaluating the proposal. Even if they are not able to simulate the view of the customer, an objective reviewer can point out inconsistencies, potential inaccuracies, ambiguities or opportunities to add content that will make the proposal more compelling. While the reviewers are reading the proposal, it is important that all contributors stop creating content; otherwise, the reviewers are reacting to content that is changing, and it can be it a waste of time for both reviewers and contributors.

Do not confuse proofreading or copy editing with reviewing. Proofreaders correct errors of spelling and grammar without changing the meaning or adding content. Copy editors look for ways to express content more succinctly and effectively, and there are multiple levels of copy editing. A deep copy edit often involves a dialogue with the authors and several iterations back and forth. When time permits, this results in a vastly superior document. Often, proposal schedules only permit a light copy edit or proofreading. But none of these activities substitute for a substantive critique of the proposal.

Reviews vary in length and complexity. Review of a short letter proposal might take one person less than an hour. Longer documents can involve

DOI: 10.4324/9781003581475-8

teams of people and last several days. As with other aspects of proposal management, context is everything, and few absolutely hard-and-fast rules exist for all situations.

Why Is it Important?

Reviews are essential because authors (and graphic artists) cannot objectively critique their own work. By definition, authors get attached to their words, and artists to their images. In fact, it is almost impossible for anyone who writes anything to see all their own errors, omissions or opportunities. The human eye can easily skip over words or phrases and, likewise, see words that are not there.

People who have not been authors bring clarity, distance and perspective. They can also perceive gaps, inconsistencies, ambiguities and inaccuracies that others closer to the proposal cannot perceive. Feedback is an essential part of creating any document, regardless of length or format.

Challenges

A proposal review can be condensed into a very short time frame if necessary, and it can also involve multiple meetings and revision cycles. The more complicated your process, the more challenges you will encounter.

The first one is the amount of time in the proposal schedule that reviews occupy. The longer the proposal document, the more time it will take. While reviewers are reading the document, contributors must stop revising or adding to the content. Otherwise, reviewers are reacting to content that might have already been revised, and their comments might no longer be relevant. This is a waste of everyone's time. After the review is complete, it takes still more time to absorb the feedback and decide how to address it. The more reviewers, the more time it takes to consolidate and make sense of the feedback, because comments can contradict each other. The proposal manager, capture manager and writers need time to discuss how to respond to the feedback and then incorporate changes. If the proposal manager schedules multiple reviews (sometimes these are not optional), each review chips away at the time available to create compelling content and edit and format the document.

The second challenge is selection of reviewers. Reviewing a proposal requires the ability to apply critical thinking and make actionable suggestions to the writers, and it represents a significant time commitment. The work involves not just reading the proposal but understanding the opportunity, the customer's environment and the solution. It can be difficult to find a reviewer who understands enough about the proposal process to make suggestions that writers can implement in a short period of time, even in large organizations with well-established processes.

A third challenge is objectivity. It is very common for reviewers to provide feedback that represents their personal opinions, but not necessarily feedback that represents the views of the customer. Furthermore, reviewers bring inherent prejudices to the job; the more senior an executive or a subject matter expert, the less likely that person is to be aware of inbuilt assumptions.

When Does it Happen?

Different organizations have different rules about how many proposal reviews to schedule and when to schedule them. It is usually a mistake to set up reviews before contributors have had a chance to create a significant amount of content (graphics, detailed outlines or text). Criticism too early in the process can be destructive to morale and is rarely constructive. At the same time, reviews should not occur too close to the proposal deadline. The proposal team needs time to understand and apply the reviewer comments.

In large organizations, there are multiple reviews, often designated by colors. A pink or red team review is a review of the proposal sections that do not contain pricing or contractual content. A blue team, which is a critique of the proposal strategy and the solution, precedes the pink team, which precedes the red team. The pricing manager usually organizes multiple green team reviews to get feedback on the pricing strategy and the final numbers. A gold team review is a review by a small number of senior executives after red team comments have been addressed. I have also seen magenta teams, yellow teams and many other variations.

The right number of reviews and their timing are context-dependent. Although they are essential, each review eats into the time available to complete the proposal. The proposal manager should discuss with the capture manager or senior executive which reviews are mandatory and which ones cannot be accommodated owing to time constraints. Achieving the balance between too little and too much feedback is one of the many judgment calls proposal managers learn to make with experience.

Who Owns it?

Different people own different aspects of the review process. The proposal manager is accountable for making sure that the reviews occur in accordance with whatever organizational policies exist. This includes scheduling and organizing the reviews and any associated logistics, distributing the proposal copy, monitoring progress, facilitating the adjudication of comments and helping the writers decide which comments to address before the next review. In some organizations, there is also an administrator who manages use of a collaborative platform that reviewers use to provide comments. Either the capture manager, the business development executive or another manager within the organization selects reviewers; often, the proposal manager collaborates on making this decision based on familiarity with the feedback provided by reviewers on past proposals.

Once the proposal and capture managers agree on the appropriate reviewers, the proposal manager is accountable for setting the dates and times for the review to start and end and developing materials to distribute to reviewers (in cooperation with the capture manager or equivalent manager), such as the RFP (and any attachments), information about the customer that would inform a review and the proposal schedule.

For the Solo Practitioner

This is the only fundamental activity for which you will need to engage someone else; all the others you can perform yourself if you have to. But, for reviews, it is essential to find someone who can be another set of eyes. No matter how well you understand what you are proposing, it is very hard to review your own content objectively. Call in a favor from a colleague or invest in professional advice from a proposal consultant.

Steps in the Process

There are nine steps to a thorough review process. They can easily be condensed and all be accomplished within several hours on proposals that have tight time constraints. But skipping any of them introduces risk.

Step 1: Select Reviewers

The first step is to select reviewers, ideally as soon as possible after receiving a final RFP. If one or more desired reviewers have busy schedules, this could affect the proposal schedule. The proposal manager is accountable for confirming who the reviewers will be, even though someone else typically makes the selection. In some organizations there are reviewers who are designated to read each proposal according to company policies, and these have to be factored in during the planning process. It is better to find out who these people are early on than to have them added to the review team at the last minute.

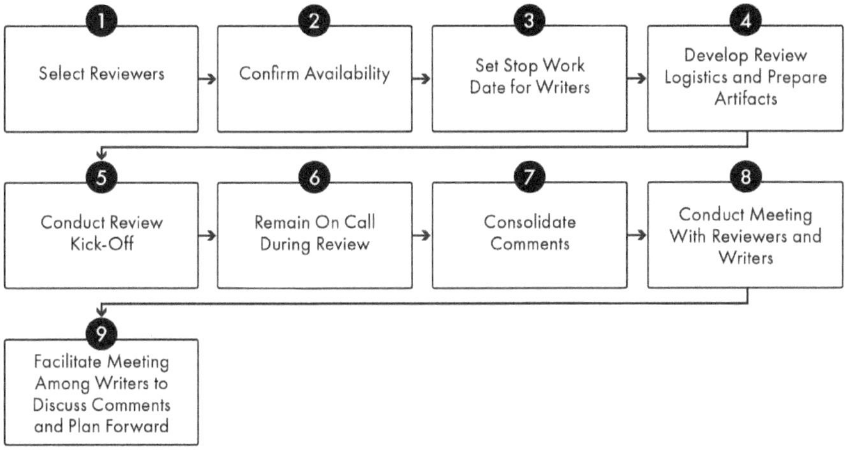

Figure 7.1 Steps in Setting Up and Conducting Reviews; It is Important to Do Them in Sequence to Avoid the Need for Rework

Many factors go into the selection of reviewers. To provide useful feedback, they should have some knowledge of the solution and of how the proposal will be read by the customer; they should also be sensitive to customer preferences and buying histories. As a practical matter, the available or required reviewers often lack this knowledge and understanding. Sometimes, they are subject matter experts who do not have time to evaluate the solution or even read the full RFP; they might be professionals from other disciplines, such as law or finance, who do not have either an understanding of the subject matter or information about the customer. This does not mean that it is a good idea to skip the review process altogether just because the perfect reviewer does not exist. An imperfect review is better than no review at all.

Each reviewer should be able to provide feedback that is based on something other than personal preferences. It might be subject matter knowledge, experience evaluating similar proposals that have been successful, insights about the customer's environment, or an ability to read carefully and identify inconsistencies or inaccuracies. As a group, the reviewers should be able to evaluate the proposal for three attributes: compliance, responsiveness and persuasiveness. Each requires explanation, since these attributes are often conflated, which causes extra work after the review.

Compliance is usually defined as whether or not the proposal is in alignment with the proposal instructions, including page count, organization, content and formatting. If the RFP states that the resumes have to be signed, and there are no signatures, this would be an example of non-compliance. However, there are situations where compliance is more nuanced. If the RFP lists requirements in a certain order, and the order they are addressed in the proposal is different, is that non-compliance? In US government RFPs, it is common to find statements such as "Bidders should explain their technical approach, methodology, processes and tools to all the PWS requirements in detail." If the proposal sections do not specifically reference every PWS requirement, is that non-compliance? For US government proposals, the answer is, it depends. Proposal managers can provide advice but should not be responsible for making these judgment calls. That is the role of the capture manager, business development manager, solution architect or senior executive.

For straightforward instructions, such as page length, compliance is extremely important because it gives the customer an easy way to disqualify a company and reduce the number of proposals that have to be evaluated. However, in the US Federal Acquisition Regulations, there is no definition of compliance, giving the contracting officers a large degree of discretion. Despite the fact that, in practice, small compliance errors, such as delivery of a proposal with a 30-page limit that has one word on page 31, which is an obvious clerical error, are overlooked, it is never worth taking the chance and risking the investment that the company has made.

Responsiveness means that the text under the heading fully and accurately addresses the topic. This involves more than repeating the requirement. Persuasiveness is the degree to which the proposal makes a convincing case for the solution being proposed. Not all reviewers will be equally adept at evaluating all three attributes. Designate at least one reviewer to check the entire document for compliance only, at each review, because content changes in between reviews. It is always a good idea for the proposal manager to also perform a complete compliance review in parallel, and it is essential to build a final compliance check into the schedule before production and delivery.

The easiest way to do this is to repurpose the table created for analyzing the RFP, described in Chapter 1, often referred to as a compliance matrix (see Table 7.1). However, the term "compliance matrix" is used in various ways in different organizations. One organization I worked with recently has a compliance matrix with more than 20 columns and includes detailed descriptions of the solution. Others are simpler. There are two basic types of compliance matrices. The first, illustrated here, is organized according to the customer's requirements; the left-hand column is a list of each requirement from each RFP document, and the other columns show where to find the requirement in the proposal. The second is organized according to proposal section; the sections are in the left-hand column, with the RFP requirements they address in the columns to the right.

Table 7.1 RFP Requirements-Driven Compliance Matrix

Requirement	*RFP Section*	*Location in Proposal*	*Compliant? Y/N*
Provide an overall management plan that identifies key personnel and the percentage of each person's time that will be committed to the project and describes the functions and responsibilities of *each* key person relative to the task to be performed	Instruction	Section 2.3.3	N Missing responsibilities for two key personnel
In addition, the management plan shall describe the experience of *all* key members	Instruction	Section 5.6.4	Y
The Proposer *must* include a description of the organizational structure and management methodology used to provide service reliability and means of coordination and communication	Instruction	Section 2.0	N No discussion of communication
The Management Team plan *shall* identify the various staffing levels, including key managerial and supervisory personnel as well as office location and operational capabilities, for *each* area of the work as described in the Scope of Services	Instruction	Section 7.4.5	Y
It *shall* clearly describe the functions and responsibilities of *each* staff member listed and *all* Subcontractors/ Subconsultants and include their experience relative to the tasks to be performed	Instruction	Section 8.4	Y

Which one to use depends on whether instructions permit the inclusion of a compliance matrix with the proposal. If they do, it is best to use the structure in Table 7.1. If not, it is helpful for reviewers to use a table organized by proposal section. In a perfect world, it is best to have both.

Step 2: Confirm Availability

The next step is to confirm the date of each review; these dates should have been established when the schedule was created. Confirm availability of all reviewers or discuss with the capture manager or senior executive the possibility of selecting different people. It is important that the review schedule remain on course because it affects all the other proposal activities, and it is better to change reviewers than to change dates.

After confirming availability, the proposal and capture managers should develop review assignments. If the proposal is short, all reviewers can read the entire document. If all the reviewers are reading the entire document, it helps to focus each reviewer. Reviewers bring different skills and perspectives that should drive their assignments. Some people are detail-oriented and are good at finding inconsistencies; others have a strategic perspective and can offer suggestions on proposal themes and structure; others can critique proposal graphics and layout. Some are especially adept at identifying risk or cost implications. For longer proposals, it makes sense to ask reviewers to focus on particular sections based on their subject matter knowledge or familiarity with the customer's situation, as long as there is at least one reviewer (ideally two or more) assigned to each proposal section.

Step 3: Set Stop Work Date for Writers

Once availability is confirmed, the proposal manager should confirm the date with all the contributors (section owners and writers) and inform them of when they will have to stop work so that the proposal can be reviewed. Typically, proposal text does not undergo a lot of formatting or editing prior to reviews that take place early in the proposal process. So, if an early review is going to begin at 8:00 am on a Monday, the writers could stop work on Friday at 8:00 am. This gives the proposal manager (and others) time to read all the proposal sections and identify any major gaps or issues. A proposal manager can flag these and save the reviewers time.

If the review is occurring close to the proposal deadline, especially if it is the last review, it helps to provide the reviewers with content that has been at least partially formatted and edited, so that the reviewers can see whether or not the document is longer than the permitted number of pages or words. Of course, this means that the writers will have to stop writing sooner to allow time for formatting and editing. The amount of time available is a zero-sum game, and this is why the decision about how many reviews to conduct and when they should be scheduled has a serious impact.

Step 4: Develop Review Logistics and Prepare Artifacts

Once there is agreement on the schedule, the proposal manager should develop review logistics, such as how reviewers should document and deliver their feedback, and then prepare a set of artifacts for the reviewers and distribute them as soon as possible. Artifacts include the proposal review assignments, the schedule for the review, the RFP and any relevant attachments, questions and answers on the RFP, and any internal documents that contain information about the customer (briefings, notes from customer calls, competitor intelligence).

Step 5: Conduct Kick Off

In many organizations, proposal managers hold a kick-off meeting for each review to explain instructions and process. This can be particularly effective if there are first-time reviewers who are new to the process. A kick-off meeting is an excellent opportunity to review the following:

- The key RFP requirements, evaluation criteria and instructions. Although it can be helpful for reviewers to read the RFP carefully front to back, this is often impractical. Part of the proposal manager's job is to distill the essence of the RFP for the reviewers. Reviewers can waste a lot of time making impractical suggestions (such as, "change the architecture so that the solution can be available on tablets and phones for all users") if they are not familiar with the details of the RFP (such as, "the only acceptable access to the application shall be through certified laptops or kiosks").
- How to document comments and suggestions. Many different approaches can work, depending on the collaborative tools available. Two common methods are the "comment" function in MS Word and the simultaneous editing function available on SharePoint sites. Many other methods can work for proposals of differing lengths and levels of complexity. Whatever the specifics of the proposal, avoid asking for handwritten comments in the margin of the page because of the challenge of reading the handwriting and aggregating comments later.
- What kinds of comments and suggestions are actionable, and what kinds will be counterproductive. Be as specific as possible. Otherwise, an inexperienced reviewer might suggest that the proposal be entirely

"You mean our proposal can only be 20 pages long? I guess I didn't read that part of the RFP. You might not be able to add all the data I provided in my next 15 slides."

rewritten, without understanding that time rarely permits this. The most actionable suggestions for a proposal review include ideas for how to add content that would make the solution more compelling, where to remove inaccuracies, which RFP requirements are missing from the proposal altogether or where details exist to substantiate claims.

- "Known" gaps. It is rare that a proposal team conducts a review of a document that is perfect, or even close to perfect. It is best to tell reviewers that certain sections have yet to be written or are known to have errors or other problems, such as grammar. Otherwise, reviewers can spend a lot of time providing feedback about problems or gaps that the proposal team already knows about. This, of course, is an ineffective use of everyone's time.
- The start and end times of the review. Typically, reviewers receive copy at a designated time and then have a certain number of days or hours to provide their feedback. Emphasize the importance of meeting review deadlines. Everyone's work expands to fill the time, and, if reviewers do not understand the high degree of dependencies inherent in a proposal schedule, they might not prioritize the task.
- Whom to contact if they have questions while reviewing the documents. This is usually, but not always, the proposal manager.
- The expectation that reviewers will be available between the date of the review and the submittal of the proposal in case there are follow-up questions.

After the kick-off meeting, the proposal manager distributes the proposal materials and is then on standby to answer questions and monitor progress. The proposal manager should contact any reviewers who do not return comments by the established deadline.

Step 6: Remain on Call During Review

While reviewers are entering their comments, the proposal manager should be on call to answer questions so that the review can stay on schedule. If the proposal manager has real-time access to reviewer comments and sees that two reviewers have opposite views of how a section should be changed, it is better to organize a phone call or meeting to discuss this before the end of the comment period so that authors do not receive conflicting advice.

Step 7: Consolidate Comments

The next step is to consolidate all the comments from the different reviewers so that authors can work from a single document. This step is not necessary if reviewers use a simultaneous editing function that is part of a collaborative tool. When there is time, it is extremely helpful to convene a meeting of the reviewers and the authors so that they can explain comments or add ideas that they did not have time to put in the document. Many people can verbally explain concepts they have trouble writing about. Authors who attend this meeting, sometimes referred to as a debrief, may resist criticism and become defensive. This is true even for experienced authors. I recommend that contributors not engage in debate with reviewers in real time and instead read the comments in detail later.

Steps 8 and 9: Conduct Meeting with Writers and Reviewers / Facilitate Meeting to Discuss Plan Forward

After the authors have had time to read all the comments, the proposal manager and capture manager should then meet with the authors to agree on how to deal with the comments. It is rare that contributors can address every suggestion, and some comments might be inappropriate. Some comments might not require a response. It helps to sort comments according to the amount of time or knowledge required to address them. Substituting one term for another is easy; changes that require hunting for data points or introducing new concepts can take a lot of time.

Sometimes, after a review, the proposal and capture managers decide that authors should be removed from the team or that they should take on different assignments. Sometimes, subject matter experts join the team of contributors. The meeting should end with everyone on the same page about how to meet the next deadline, whether it is the next review or the final "pens down" before formatting and production.

Conclusion

Reviews, although essential, eat into the schedule and drive up the proposal cost. It is difficult to take a short cut or skip steps in the process without creating additional challenges. It is too easy to generate feedback that authors cannot understand or use, which only adds to schedule pressures and can often lead to poor morale across the team. Early discussions about the available reviewers, as well as how best to engage them, and careful planning are the best tools to get the most out of reviews and avoid inefficiencies. One good, thorough proposal critique is better than a series of partial reviews by people who provide feedback that authors cannot use.

Chapter 8

Production and Delivery

Definition

Production consists of making final changes and then either printing onto paper or populating a website, removable drive or other format for electronic delivery. Delivery entails not just sending the proposal but also getting written confirmation that the customer received it.

Why Is it Important?

Time spent planning for production and delivery will pay off in the final days or hours. If you don't budget for this, people will underestimate the time required for these final and essential steps.

Challenges

Production and delivery are the very last steps in the proposal process and, for that reason, they carry with them significant risks. They can appear simple and straightforward to someone who does not produce documents for a living, and this creates the impression that they can be done very quickly. In fact, they can be complicated and time-consuming. Because they occur at the end of the process, they have to be done by a deadline that cannot be extended; this is what creates the risk. If a file is corrupted or a driver cannot find the correct address at the last moment, there might not be enough time to fix the problem, in which case the proposal arrives late, and all the work to create the proposal will have been squandered. Although some contracts and grants operate on a "rolling admissions" basis, in most situations, a late proposal is immediately disqualified.

These last steps can be as simple as proofreading answers you have entered into an online form and pressing a button to submit the proposal. But they can involve, in addition to proofreading, copy editing, desktop publishing, cross-referencing, indexing, standardization of graphics and colors, changing margins or fonts, adding headers and footers, attaching

DOI: 10.4324/9781003581475-9

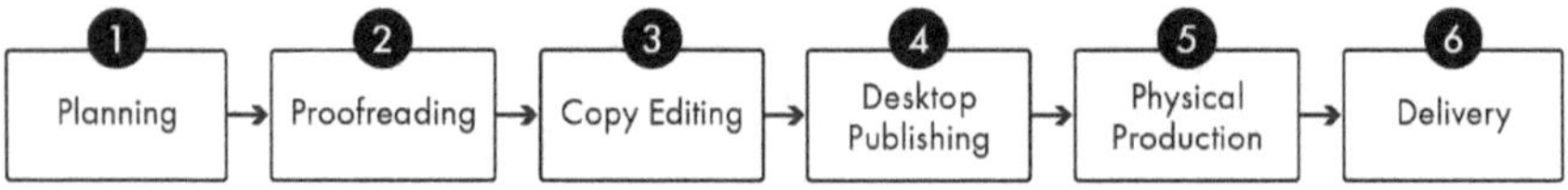

Figure 8.1 Steps in Production and Delivery; the Planning Step is the Most Critical

covers, adding acronym lists and other attachments, creating tables of contents, inserting cover art, burning CDs, printing, assembling books with sections separated by tabs, binding, packing, wrapping and physical delivery. Delivery might consist of a click on a keyboard but, often, there are booby traps such as limitations on file size and slow networks. RFPs often include extremely specific formatting and delivery instructions, which means that few production and delivery rules apply in all situations. But some overarching principles are relevant, regardless of the RFP.

When Does it Happen?

Production and delivery occur after all reviews, compliance checks and content changes to the document are complete.

Who Owns it?

The proposal manager is accountable for making sure these steps get done within the time allocated for them. Others do the work and participate in the planning.

Steps in the Process

These steps are in sequential order; performing them out of order is likely to create the need for reworking and threaten the proposal schedule and on-time delivery.

Step 1: Planning

Budgeting the right amount of time and allocating the right people for production and delivery are part of creating realistic proposal assignments and a workable schedule. In a perfect world, professional editors, proofreaders, formatters and graphic artists all play a role so that the production schedule is based on expert knowledge of how long production tasks actually take. Sometimes, the proposal schedule does not permit a full copy edit, hand delivery or professional binding, and it is necessary to compress or even eliminate steps. When the team has a week to prepare a proposal, it is not realistic to plan for extensive copy editing.

As soon as final RFP instructions are available, proposal managers should define production standards and determine which steps are required for successful production and delivery given the time and expense constraints. Over-engineering can be as dangerous as not planning at all. Determine the start time and the duration for each activity and document the plan. It is important to get consensus early on as to which steps are necessary versus optional, from senior managers and other stakeholders, well before you enter the production phase. If a senior executive insists on heavy copy editing and professional photographs, it is the proposal manager's responsibility to document the additional time and expense involved. Early buy-in prevents random stakeholders from weighing in on details about the appearance of the proposal when there is no time or budget to accommodate changes, resulting in the introduction of errors or late delivery. The plan should also include the names of a small number of people who will be checking the document after editing and formatting.

Other planning activities include setting up a document template with the correct format, defining standard terms, establishing rules about forward and backward references and reminding authors of best practices for inserting or deleting content and preserving version control.

Once the plan is complete, create a checklist that includes both the required items from the RFP as well as the ones that are desirable but not absolutely necessary (Table 8.1).

Table 8.1

Activity	*Who*	*Timing*
Check/correct margins	Desktop publisher	Begin after formatting is complete
Check/correct font size/text	Desktop publisher	
Check/correct font size/graphics	Desktop publisher	
Check/correct pagination	Desktop publisher	
Check/correct cover page content	Proposal manager	
Check final page count	Desktop publisher	
	High Priority	
Standardize color palette	Desktop publisher	No later than 1 day prior to delivery
Check captions for graphics	Proposal manager	
Check cross-references	Desktop publisher	
Create table of contents	Desktop publisher	
Proofread	Editor	
	If Time Permits	
Insert acronym list	Proposal manager	No later than 1 day prior to delivery
Light copy edit	Editor	No later than 1 day prior to delivery

Planning for production also means testing any hardware or software you will be using, ordering supplies (binders, divider tables, coil binding, acetate, heavy-duty paper, plastic sleeves, packing boxes and tape) and checking on licenses for any software the team might need for formatting or graphics.

Step 2: Proofreading

This means correcting basic spelling and grammar errors and standardizing spelling, punctuation, use of upper versus lower case ("the Government" or "the government"?) and treatment of acronyms. Proofreading is much easier if the proposal manager builds a list of terminology and develops standards before the production phase. Although automated tools exist, proofreading remains a manual exercise because most tools cannot distinguish incorrect use of words such as "affect" versus "effect." No matter how short the proposal or how limited the time, do not skip this step.

Step 3: Copy Editing

This is often confused with proofreading and even formatting. Yet it is quite distinct. Some editors proofread as well as edit, but most proofreaders do not have the skill or experience to copy edit. Copy editing occurs on a scale, depending on how much time is available and how experienced the editor is. A light copy edit consists of eliminating redundant words and clichés, shortening sentences to save space and checking for consistency in use of terminology. A deep copy edit consists of rewording sentences to increase clarity and remove redundant or vague language. It can also mean changing the order of sentences within a paragraph, or paragraphs within a proposal section. Copy editors are often able to cut significant amounts of text without changing the meaning, an advantage when the RFP has strict page limits. Good copy editing is invaluable, because writers themselves are too close to the text to be able to see how it could be improved. However, copy editing takes time, as much as 30 minutes per page for dense or technical material. The editing process is

> **For the Solo Practitioner**
>
> Isolate time when you are not thinking about content to proofread, edit and format. For many short proposals, especially grant proposals, this phase is not taxing. It is important to address it after you have made all the final decisions about the content of your proposal.

iterative. Editors are not subject matter experts, so they often have questions about the changes they are proposing ("Did you mean to say 'Project Manager' here, because all the other references are to a 'Program Manager'?"). Once the queries are answered, if writers introduce new copy, that copy has to be edited as well. This is one reason that deep copy editing occurs at the end of the process. However, there is a counter-argument to waiting until the end. If the document is not well written, it is difficult for reviewers to understand the content and provide meaningful feedback. When this happens, instead of reviewing the proposal for content, they spend their time fixing grammar and syntax. Ultimately, the decision about how deep an edit to plan for and when to schedule it comes down to how much time there is to execute all the other steps. Sometimes, a preliminary edit for readability before a review is followed by a deep copy edit after the review.

Step 4: Desktop Publishing

This step determines the appearance of your proposal. Proposal managers have an obligation to deliver a document that looks as professional as possible. At the same time, we are constrained by time, budgets and people. A natural tension exists between attention to the content and the appearance of the proposal because both are important, and often one comes at the expense of the other.

The minimal standard for desktop publishing is formatting the proposal in accordance with the instructions in the RFP as to font, margins, paper size, orientation or other production values. Proposal managers typically exceed what is required and instruct the desktop publishers to standardize the page layout, including all the headings, captions, text boxes, headers and footers, fonts, margins, page numbering and cross-references; to name the files consistently; and to insert tables of contents, indexes, covers, acronym lists, the latest version of all graphics or illustrations, and appendices or attachments. Some formatting typically occurs early in the proposal process because, without the correct fonts or margins, it is impossible to know the actual length of the document. But the final formatting comes at the very end, and, once it is done, writers should not add new content or change the text. For this reason, the version of the proposal that is sent to reviewers is often only partially formatted. Otherwise, the changes proposed by reviewers result in another cycle of desktop publishing.

Although desktop publishing tools are accessible to writers and appear to be easy to use, it makes sense to engage a professional to do the final formatting. It is worth the investment because professionals can work quickly and accurately. Amateurs typically know just enough to be dangerous and, with one or two incorrect key strokes, they can introduce errors that corrupt the document and take professional desktop publishers hours to undo. If you cannot engage a professional in time to meet the proposal deadline, be sure to find one before your next proposal through referrals from colleagues or online markets where freelancers offer their services.

If you have to be your own desktop publisher, keep the document structure as simple as possible. Multiple layers of numbered headings, elaborate graphics or cross-references, or complicated headers or footers can send you down a rabbit hole and eat up valuable time better spent on the content of the proposal.

Regardless of whether you have to deliver a printed proposal, create a hard copy of the formatted document and check it carefully for errors. It is easy to miss formatting errors when reviewing on a screen.

Step 5: Physical Production

If you have to deliver a printed proposal or an electronic proposal on media such as DVDs or thumb drives, overestimate the amount of time it will take to print and bind the documents, assemble the pages into binders or burn CDs and prepare packages for shipping. These activities always take longer than they should, even if you have been scrupulous about maintaining the printer and you have all the supplies you need close at hand. If everything is working perfectly, printing several hundred pages and assembling them into notebooks goes quickly. Often, everything does not work perfectly. Formatting errors appear on the printed page that were not visible on the screen. Paper jams. Notebook rings do not open or close properly. Ink cartridges run dry. The power goes out owing to an electrical storm. The printer malfunctions. The list of potential problems is long. Even though the likelihood appears low, the potential consequences of any one of these events could be disastrous, because any one of them could result in missing the deadline, which means all the work leading up to the production of the proposal was in vain.

If you have to deliver soft copy on a disk or thumb drive, allow time to create the necessary files and folders on the device and then check each one on a different computer. Print one hard copy and make sure it is perfect before you burn CDs or transfer files to a thumb drive.

Print shops can cut down on the risk, since they usually have staff on hand to manage technical problems, but the risk of late delivery goes up when you turn over control to an outside firm unless you are confident of their ability to meet strict deadlines. If you can test drive a print shop with a project that does not have a hard deadline, you can gauge how reliable they will be when you use them for proposal production. If you turn over physical production to another department or a print shop, provide specific instructions and establish a deadline in advance of the time you need the documents for delivery. Provide the print shop with a "go-by" book. This is a sample of what the final volume(s) will look like that includes each page of the proposal, with the different sections in the correct order, separated by tabs if necessary. Make sure the print shop knows the file name(s) that correspond to each section of the proposal.

Step 6: Delivery

The simplest form of delivery is an email attachment or an upload to a website. Do not wait until five minutes before the time the proposal is due. You might find that the file is too large, that the website is not available or that the internet is down. In-person delivery is subject to many more contingencies: no one is there to accept delivery, gridlock on the roads, bad weather or delays in commercial courier deliveries, at a minimum. The best way to minimize the risk associated with a physical delivery is to get as much information as possible about who is going to receive the proposal and the exact location and access requirements, particularly if the location is on government property, well in advance. Always find out whether the delivery person will have to show identification and ask what hours the building will be open. Get the phone and email contact information for the recipient. Double-check driving directions because electronic navigation systems can malfunction. Whether you use a courier, hand delivery, email or another form of electronic delivery, whoever delivers should insist on acknowledgment of receipt.

Conclusion: Adhere to the Plan and Enforce Single Control

Stick to the milestones established in the production plan. With amendments and extensions, there is always the risk you will have to move a deadline, but, the more times you change the schedule, the less credibility you have. Once you enter the production and delivery phase, one person should own each activity (proofreading, editing, formatting), and the rest of the proposal team should either stay away or take direction from that one person. After editing and formatting, do not continue to engage more than a few people to review the document for errors. For those who do conduct this final review, limit changes to text or graphics to glaring errors that involve accuracy (such as 20 million instead of 2 million) or statements that could create risk during execution. Designate one person who will have access to the native file to make the change. The fewer people who touch the document during the production and delivery phase, the better. There is no perfect proposal; improvement in the text, the graphics, the appearance, the cover is always possible. The instinct to continue to make changes is difficult to fight. However, the more people tweak the document, the higher the risk of missing the deadline, because a tiny change in one place can ripple across the proposal and have unintended consequences. Moreover, last-minute changes are often the result of dedicated SMEs or executives rethinking earlier decisions and introducing errors in judgment or fact, when they would have been better served by leaving well enough alone. Experienced proposal managers know when to stop work and how to resist demands for last-minute changes.

"We cannot submit a proposal with this color scheme and I also don't like the font. It won't take that long to make some other changes as well. Besides, we have very fast printers."

Chapter 9

Daily Proposal Management and Communication with the Team

The functions in this chapter are closely related to, and embedded in, all proposal activities, from RFP shredding to final reviews. These are activities you should be doing daily. They are the regular rituals that can seem formal and time-consuming, until you see what happens when you decide not to do them. To keep a proposal running smoothly, there are some minimum daily requirements: (1.) scanning any incoming information to determine its impact on the proposal schedule and content, (2.) broadcasting messages to the proposal team, (3.) learning what progress has been made on each proposal section, (4.) responding to inquiries, (5.) resolving problems or escalating them to a level where they can be resolved, (6.) running a daily status meeting, (7.) documenting any new decisions or information and (8.) managing your own time based on changing priorities. Because they are ongoing, I am not presenting a series of steps but, rather, principles and tools to help in executing each function. This is the daily blocking and tackling that will enable you to keep to a schedule and deliver a winning proposal, without all-nighters, without heroics, without excessive stress. In executing them, be intentional and deliberate. It is easy to slide into casual behavior patterns, but, for these functions, a more formal approach pays many dividends.

Scanning Incoming Information

The proposal manager is often the person at the receiving end of formal and informal messages, whether through emails from the customer, phone calls, hallway conversations or written communications. Typically, only the proposal manager and the capture manager see all the incoming traffic. The proposal manager has to stay on top of everything that comes in. By "stay on top," I mean understand what the message is about, not necessarily the implications of all the details. If you receive technical material or messages containing complicated legal or financial language, and you cannot tell what the implications are, find someone who can interpret for you.

DOI: 10.4324/9781003581475-10

Ask that person to explain why the information is or is not important. Over time, if you continue to manage proposals for the same customer, you will become familiar with the language and will be able to assess it for yourself. Whatever you do, resist the temptation to set aside things you do not understand. There could be something buried in an amendment or an answer to your question that will make a large difference to the solution or the price, or even the company's ability to bid. A complicated RFP amendment might contain 50 pages of contractual boilerplate that does not affect either the proposal or the execution of the work; it might also contain a clause that could put the future of the company at risk. It is not the job of the proposal manager to make that determination; the responsibility of the proposal manager is to make sure a competent expert reviews those 50 pages to determine the implications.

Staying on top of everything does not mean that it is essential to immediately transmit every data point to every participant. Participants are often already on information overload and, if they receive too much mail, they start to ignore all of it or pay attention only randomly. So, triage is essential. An excellent example is hearsay from a business development or capture executive that the proposal deadline "might" be extended. Until the deadline actually is extended formally, this knowledge is not valuable to the team and can just aggravate existing tendencies to procrastinate. On the other hand, if the proposal manager receives answers to questions that reverse the team's understanding of the RFP requirements, it is important to share them quickly with anyone whose work relates to those requirements. Such answers might dictate the need for additional solution sessions, graphics, pricing calculations or legal reviews.

Broadcasting Messages to the Proposal Team

A broadcast message is a one-way communication from the proposal manager that does not require a response. Broadcast messages are common at the beginning of the process to explain the proposal schedule, the location of files, high-level roles and responsibilities, and proposal writing instructions. During the life of the proposal, broadcast messages provide the team with new and relevant information. This might be a simple transmission of a document received, or it might be a message about the schedule, content or format of the proposal. Being clear and concise is essential and, although this sounds obvious and simple, it is neither. The opportunities for miscommunication, as well as missed communication, are endless, and remote work has only increased these dangers. This topic could easily fill another book, and, although many business communication books exist, most do not address the specific types of communication that are relevant in our deadline-driven business. What follows is only a brief discussion of some of the essential points.

Assess the channels available for reaching your team. They might include in-person meetings, teleconferences, video conferences, email, chat or instant messaging (IM), text messages (these have different attributes from instant messages, so be sure you understand the limitations of each), shared documents on a platform or voicemail messages. Identify how you want to use these channels and use them consistently. Otherwise, people will be waiting for a voicemail when, instead, they should be logging into the portal. Channels are not mutually exclusive; I often have to communicate the same information through multiple channels to make sure that it is received and understood. Proposal team members are often juggling multiple commitments, and one conversation or message is frequently not enough.

As part of your proposal kick-off, explain to the team how you are going to structure your broadcast communications. Email and IM tend to be the preferred methods despite the high likelihood of misinterpretation. Another option is to ask all participants to check a collaboration space once a day at a specified time, sending an automatically generated text message or voicemail reminding them to do so. If your team is used to unstructured communication, a formal process will require adjustment. This is a challenge that proposal managers should address head-on at the beginning of the process, because excessive reliance on email will create the need for reworking through misunderstandings and hours lost trying to locate messages and files that might have been attached. A daily call, discussed below, is another way to deliver broadcast messages. However, if you rely exclusively on a call, your message will probably not get to everyone because people occasionally have to miss the call.

Since most organizations are wedded to email and overly dependent on it as a form of workflow, I have developed a simple rule for limiting its use on proposals: I use email only for structured, scheduled and predictable transmissions, such as the daily digest described later in this chapter, or for content that people need to know about in real time, as long as that content consists of unambiguous statements of facts. For example:

- The deadline for proposal delivery has been extended until Thursday, June 25 at 5:00 pm EDT;
- The noon meeting has been canceled;
- The SharePoint site will be down for scheduled maintenance Saturday between 12:00 am and 6:00 am.

Anything that is more complicated or nuanced I communicate through a different channel, often a phone call, a teleconference with multiple people or an update to a document on a collaborative platform. I also ask people to use a subject line that reflects the content of the message, such as "DoJ Helpdesk Proposal/Missing Subcontractor Data/Action Required." I limit the use of email attachments to messages for people outside the firewall who cannot access a collaborative site and request that everyone on the team follow that practice. This does require an organized file structure on your team site or collaborative tool so that people know where to upload and where to find files.

IM is especially dangerous because there is no audit trail. Instant messages often disappear on logout. So, if someone drops the ball, it can be difficult to find out what happened and why, if all the communication occurred through an IM platform. IM is best for messages that will become immediately obsolete, such as "Hi, we have started the meeting. Are you going to join the call?"

Even with a deliberate and intentional communication plan, there will always be some ad hoc phone calls, emails and other messages. This is unavoidable in a fast-moving environment. Flexibility is just as critical as structure. The goal is to keep ad hoc broadcast communications to a

Table 9.1 Proposal Communication Plan

Information or Artifact	*Cadence, Location, Access*
RFP, amendments, answers to questions on the RFP, proposal schedule, proposal outline, contact list, action item list	Posted on GoogleDrive; all have access
Drafts of the proposal	In labeled folders on GoogleDrive; authors and proposal content owners have access
Responses to data calls to subcontractors	In labeled folder on GoogleDrive; proposal manager, capture manager, subcontracts manager and pricing team have access
Meeting invitations	Sent via email
Assumptions	In a document on GoogleDrive; updates only with the permission of the proposal manager and capture manager
Notification of amendments or additional answers to questions	Sent via email when they occur; files posted to a folder on GoogleDrive
Writing assignments and instructions	Originally discussed in 1:1 meetings; documented in files posted to GoogleDrive; section owners and proposal manager have access
Proposal status	Discussed during daily call; summarized daily at COB in daily digest which is emailed to the entire team

minimum and make them the exception, not the norm. If we apply some simple rules about cadence with content and access, a typical communication plan might look something like Table 9.1.

Develop a strategy for how much information you are going to share with which people. Are you going to share everything with everyone? Is there going to be a core group that gets one level of information and a larger group that only receives more limited information? If you have a large team that includes senior executives, it might not be appropriate or efficient to copy them in on communications about tactical details. Subcontractors often do not need the same amount of information as team members in the prime contractor organization. My personal preference is to share as much as possible with as many people as possible, because it reduces the housekeeping associated with multiple levels of access. However, proposal managers often process sensitive data such as salaries or designs that are classified or proprietary, so it is likely you will not be able to share everything all the time. Implementing your communications strategy depends on having an up-to-date contact list, an administrative task that it is easy to overlook, but one that constitutes one of the proposal manager's core responsibilities. Establish your list at the beginning of the process and make sure that you update it each time someone new joins the team.

A communication schedule and cadence are equally important. A constant stream of emails, phone calls and meetings constitutes overload, and team members will start to ignore them or they will not have time to execute their proposal functions. If you try to keep everyone informed 24/7, you will probably never catch up. On the other hand, failure to notify people of critical developments will undermine confidence and morale. People will start to question your organizational skills and competence to get them to the finish line. Striking the right balance comes with practice. If you are unsure, ask for advice from the people on the team who participated in proposals in the past. As with your communication strategy, there is no one communication schedule that is ideal in all situations, and the only wrong way is to not have one at all. Once you establish a schedule, stick to it. Otherwise, you create unnecessary confusion and churn because people are expecting a communication and do not know if it was not transmitted, if it was delayed or if it was lost in cyberspace.

It is impossible and impractical to schedule and structure every message, conversation, phone call or chat. The proposal environment is dynamic, and things can change moment to moment. However, if we do not apply any discipline at all to our communications, the result is what Cal Newport, Georgetown University professor and productivity expert, describes as: "ongoing conversations fueled by unstructured and unscheduled messages."[1] The danger of this unstructured approach might not be evident, but Newport has done the research and concludes that, "In the moment, the ability to quickly delegate tasks or solicit feedback might seem like an act of streamlining, but ... in the long run, it's likely reducing productivity, requiring more time ... to get the same total amount of work accomplished."

Although it makes more work for the proposal manager, a written daily report of important events and decisions is a useful tool for keeping large proposal teams informed and on schedule. I call mine the "daily digest" and I transmit it at the end of each day. It summarizes the major events of the day and follow-up.

I created this initially for my own use during my first experience working with a 100% remote team and then began sending it to my team. The positive response surprised me. That team and subsequent ones told me I was the best proposal manager they had ever encountered (really?)! To me, it seemed elemental. But it tapped into a deep-seated need for structure and a sense of relief that there was one standard, predictable communication each day that everyone could rely on as the single source of truth in a chaotic world of cascading messages and emails. Because large proposals tend to last for longer periods of time, there have been evenings when I could not publish a digest. In those instances, I let everyone know that the digest would be published in the morning and I made sure to follow through the next day, or I simply told the team that there would be no digest that day.

Assessing Progress

Measuring progress daily is the only way to know whether you will meet the deadlines you have set in your schedule. Progress can take multiple forms: a signed teaming agreement with a subcontractor, pages of proposal

CSTiP Proposal Daily Digest (10/16/2019)

Action	Follow-Up
Discussion of technical volume content, crosswalk with PWS, and transition plan between Sam and Susan	On track to have copy posted over the weekend for review
Kick off contracts and price volume – thank you to Richelle for walking us through these volumes	Pricing will draft an additional question to submit to the government
Pink team copy due NOON on Tuesday 10/22	Roger, Sally, Jack, Wendy to post to folder on VPC – shown below in notes section of this document
New team member: Mo Simons; discussion between him and Wendy about content and format as well as schedule	Mo is Book boss for technical volume (volume III)
Pink team plans: those participating, plan to start at 8am both days and bring your laptop	More details on the Pink team to follow

Figure 9.1 Sample Daily Report

text and graphics, revisions to pricing spreadsheets, approvals and receipt of feedback on proposal sections. In the pre-digital, pre-work-from-home era, it was common to assess progress by posting proposal content onto a wall and "walking the wall" every morning. Although this is no longer practical for most organizations, digital collaboration tools enable the proposal manager to see exactly who has created and edited documents and when. Once you have set up a collaborative site, you can establish automatic notifications when files are edited, generate regular reports that show activity in each folder or manually check each proposal document to assess status. Typically, an unchanged file or folder means that there has been no progress or that people are working offline and not updating the file. Either one constitutes an issue that the proposal manager has to address.

Although my standard agenda for a daily call includes an update from each section owner, I do not rely exclusively on that update. For proposal sections, the true measure of progress is the content that has been created or revised. Be sure to keep writers informed as to the timing of the next review and your expectations for further changes or additional text, as well as any deadlines that affect their participation in the proposal. This might mean sending messages through multiple channels for redundancy. Although redundancy implies inefficiency, lack of communication often has serious consequences

Assessing progress in proposal activities that involve negotiation, approvals or analysis is more nuanced. Often, these activities do not have discrete artifacts that you can check to measure how much has been accomplished. The daily call is one way to check progress on proposal activities that do not necessarily generate a specific artifact. But the owners of these activities – typically, human resources, contracts, legal, finance, security – should each develop their own schedules and status calls to monitor progress.

Responding to Inquiries

Incoming inquiries can expand to fill many hours of a proposal manager's day. Some are likely to be simple, factual questions that can be answered in real time in a phone call or at the daily status meeting. Others might involve research, coordination with senior executives, discussion with subject matter experts or convening of meetings, all of which take time. Although it might be possible to postpone some answers or refer contributors elsewhere, it is the proposal manager's responsibility to respond as quickly as possible. Delays can result in stalled progress and missed deadlines. The best way to curtail the number of questions is to explain the proposal outline, schedule, roles and processes as clearly as possible at the beginning. If requests for information and clarification are taking up most of your day,

"I haven't heard from the proposal manager since I sent in my draft, so I am taking the rest of the month off and turning off my cell phone."

it means that you have not successfully completed or explained some of the other activities in this book. It is worth revisiting the outline, schedule, solution, assignments and review process so that you can reduce the amount of time you spend answering phone calls and emails.

Resolving or Escalating Problems

Unresolved issues will quickly sabotage the proposal schedule. You can compile a list of issues from discussions on the daily status call, your own observations as a proposal manager regarding progress on proposal sections, inconsistencies you observe through email traffic or meetings, and miscommunications and misunderstandings that inevitably arise in electronic communications. It is rare to get through an entire day without any issues at all. So, if you are not observing any, you might not be doing a good job of assessing progress. If you redouble your efforts to find out the status of each proposal activity or section and do not find any issues, consider yourself lucky, for that day, and do not create any. A proposal manager who ignores or fails to see potential problems is not acting responsibly, but, on the other hand, a "Chicken Little" proposal manager who sees crises everywhere loses credibility and creates unnecessary stress for executives and contributors. This is a balance that you learn over time.

The number one issue on most proposals is the absence of measurable progress on proposal sections. Although a proposal manager can use the daily call to discuss stalled progress, it is usually unproductive to call people out by name. Often, the contributors are senior subject matter experts who are contributing their time at the cost of fulfilling other commitments, and naming them in a public forum will create hostility that you will not be able to overcome. Stalled progress is usually best addressed in one-to-one meetings with the section owner, but, often, the proposal manager has to escalate to an executive who can conduct such a meeting. Escalation provides the proposal manager with a useful buffer from a potentially resentful contributor, but do not escalate and then drop it. The person you escalate to owes you an answer and a resolution, or recommendation for a different course of action, and the issue remains open and the responsibility of the proposal manager until there is evidence that it has been closed.

Additional "garden variety" proposal issues include:

- Incorrect version control;
- Inability to find files or folders in a collaborative workspace;
- Personality differences and friction;
- Non-responsiveness by one or more participants;
- Proposal participants who do not have the skills or knowledge needed to execute their function;
- Not enough graphics;
- Too much re-use from previous proposals;
- Insufficient insight into customer preferences;
- Changes to the proposal outline.

Running Daily Status Meetings

Status meetings are just one channel for communicating with the team, but they merit separate discussion because they are fundamental to the success of your proposal. Like the foundation of a house, they provide stability and durability. There are many arguments against daily meetings, and it is tempting to cancel them, combine them with other meetings or schedule them two or three times a week rather than daily. No one wants more meetings, and there will be days when there is nothing significant to discuss in the status meeting. Daily meetings might seem like a waste of time for a "bit" player. Contributors want to attend meetings that seem like a good use of their time, not ones where most of the information discussed is not relevant to them. On any given day, a participant might not learn any new information or raise any concerns.

Despite these objections, which sound logical, professional and successful proposal managers are religious about daily status calls. There are multiple reasons for this.

First, the muscle memory of calling in (or showing up) each day unites the team and creates accountability.

Second, the call provides the proposal manager an efficient way to send a broadcast message to the entire team in real time. Events occur during a proposal that dictate a change in the solution, the subcontractors, the pricing strategy or the staffing. Customers answer questions and amend the RFP, subcontractors join or leave the team, and subject matter experts refine the solution. When a subcontractor leaves the team or a contributor has a personal emergency, it is usually important to get the word out fast. Otherwise, people waste their time working on incorrect assumptions and then face the task of rewriting proposal sections. Without a regularly scheduled daily status call, the proposal manager has to rely on email, instant messaging, voicemails, updates to documents on a collaborative site or multiple meetings just to inform the team about recent events. A broadcast message on a short daily call is by far the most efficient way to keep everyone up-to-date.

Third, the meeting is one way for the proposal manager to learn which proposal sections are on track and which need immediate attention. If you train yourself to facilitate these meetings in the style of an agile software scrum, in which each section owner reports on progress in the past 24 hours and plans for the next 24 hours, you will have a good snapshot of how close you are to meeting the next proposal milestone.

Fourth, the daily call enables each member of the team to become aware of interdependencies. Every part of the proposal relates in some way to every other part. A change in one section will ripple across and affect other players. Suppose, for example, the customer issues a revised RFP that changes the specifications for the solution. This can affect the price, the proposed staffing plan, the subcontractors or vendors required, the past performance or references, among other proposal sections. A desktop publisher might think that the daily status meetings are a waste of time because the desktop publishing task occurs late in the process and seems unrelated to the solution, the strategy, the pricing and the subcontracting, until an amended RFP includes the requirement that the proposal be submitted in a specific format that is not consistent with the standard template. Or the due date is extended until three days after the desktop publisher has left for vacation. If people work in silos and do not share information daily, some of the "bit players" are angry that they have not been kept in the loop. As an aside, there is no such thing as a "bit player" on a proposal. The desktop publisher is every bit as important as the solution architect and, on some days, more important.

The most effective status meetings are short (ideally they take no more than 15 minutes) and at the same time every day. Some teams prefer a meeting at the end of the business day to prepare for the next day; others prefer one in the morning or at noon. As long as the time is the same every day, do what is best for the team. On very fast-moving proposals, you might want to schedule one call early in the day and one call mid- to late-afternoon. Effective status meetings start on time and end on time. Encourage participants to identify any problems that might be getting in their way, but discourage them from trying to solve all but the simplest problems during the status meeting. Keep track of the items that require separate meetings and summarize them at the end of the status meeting.

On my proposals, everyone who has any role in the proposal attends the status meetings, no matter how small the role. If you have a lot of participants, and many of them are participating via teleconferencing, ask everyone to dial in several minutes in advance. Otherwise, either the meeting starts late, which makes it difficult to keep to the 15 minutes, or it starts on time, and no one can hear what is being said because of the beep each time someone joins the call.

A standard agenda keeps the meeting on track. A typical agenda might resemble the following:

8:00–8:02 Announcements about the RFP, solution, staffing, or schedule
8:02–8:10 Status of each major proposal section (delivered by the person who owns the section)
8:10–8:12 Summary of issues to be addressed offline, with identification of the people responsible for next steps
8:12–8:15 Questions from the team

The last agenda item, reserving time for people to ask questions or raise concerns, is critical. Otherwise, progress will stall, and the proposal manager will not know why. The daily call provides a platform for anyone who cannot move forward, for whatever reason (technical challenges, lack of information, non-response by senior executives, confusion as to file location), to speak up; it thereby reinforces accountability, because it is understood that, if a person does not speak up, the assumption is that there will be measurable progress.

The daily call, in short, is one way to learn about progress, resolve issues, broadcast messages and answer inquiries. You can get a snapshot of each proposal section. You can answer routine or factual questions. You can resolve simple issues. But, if you rely on the daily call as the only way to accomplish all the tasks in this chapter, you will have very long meetings, probably with spotty attendance. You will not have an accurate picture of what progress has been made or a good understanding of why progress has stopped.

Documentation

Storing and updating proposal documents are key responsibilities of the proposal manager. The RFP, schedule, outline and proposal draft should be available to the team and easy to locate at all times. But those artifacts alone are not sufficient if the RFP or the subcontractors or the proposed personnel change. Those artifacts are not sufficient if a senior executive reviews the proposal late in the process and wants to introduce changes, or if there is a long delay in the procurement and the proposal team is dispersed. For these contingencies, it is important to have a record that a new team can use to resume work, explain decisions or troubleshoot problems. Every experienced proposal manager has been in a meeting when no one can answer questions such as, "Why did we decide to lower our price by $20M?," "Who told the Acme Spectrometer Company that their product did not meet specifications?" or "Why did we delete Figure RTS0012?"

A few standard artifacts, such as a contact list, are relevant for all proposals; others have to be developed based on the specifics of the bid. My rule of thumb is to document as much as possible without having record-keeping expand to fill all the available time. I document almost everything that will not be obsolete within a few hours. We already reviewed the importance of documenting the solution; if it changes, you should update any engineering drawings, lists of specifications, diagrams or text that explain the solution. If an important discussion or decision takes place through email, extract the text from the email thread and file it. Create a file to capture assumptions you are making as you develop the proposal and the solution. All communications with the customer belong in one folder. Create additional folders for previous proposals, data about the competition, customer-generated documents, subcontractor data call responses, style sheets, instructions to writers and briefings to senior executives. The goal is to be able to recover from the "dead man at lunch" contingency: this means that, if one person disappears from the team with no advance notice, everyone else can keep working. (The "dead man at lunch" phrase is, of course, a nostalgic reminder of the days when people actually went out to lunch.) My daily digest serves the purpose of communicating as well as documenting and it has been an invaluable reference.

Managing Your Time and Planning Your Day

Every proposal manager's day is a mix of all the activities discussed in this and previous chapters. But deciding what to focus on in any given moment can be challenging. Often, this results in "management by inbox," which means that the proposal manager is lurching from one crisis to the next. I recommend instead that you budget your time according to established criteria, with the understanding that there will, on occasion, be emergencies that require reallocation of the available time. My own priorities include:

- Items with long lead times;
- Items with near term deadlines;
- Items that enable others to execute their tasks.

If you schedule your day so that each 20-, 30-, 40- or 50-minute block of time is allocated to a specific task, you are much more likely to make progress than if you simply react to events in real time. Initially, planning your day takes work, because you probably do not have enough experience in tracking your time to know how long a given task is going to take. If the first task of the day takes twice as long as you budgeted, do not throw out the idea of planning. Re-plan the day with the available hours. If you follow this practice, you will get better at estimating the time for each task. Do not schedule every single minute, because there are always interruptions and unanticipated events. Breaks are important as well; no one is productive hour after hour, and too much exertion results in not only diminishing returns but also the introduction of errors.

Conclusion

Daily proposal management should be intentional. Do not try to "wing it." The stakes are too high. If you are deliberate, it will initially take more time, but it will pay you back many times over. People need structure, predictability and consistency in order to be productive on any task, and it is the responsibility of the proposal manager to bring these to the process.

Notes

1 Cited in "What's a World without Email 'For the Entrepreneur and Small Businessperson,'" Forbes Online Newsletter, March 9, 2021; https://www.forbes.com/sites/nishacharya/2021/03/09/whats-a-world-without-email-for-the-entrepreneur-and-small-businessperson/

Index

Note: **Bold** page numbers refer to tables and boxes and page numbers followed by "n" denote endnotes.

FSC
www.fsc.org
MIX
Papier | Fördert gute Waldnutzung
FSC® C083411

Kolibri 360 GmbH
Ferdinand-Jühlke-Straße 7
99095 Erfurt, Deutschland
produktsicherheit@kolibri360.de